SHEFFIELD HALLAM UNIVERSITY
LEARNING CENTRE
COLLEGIATE CRESCENT CAMPUS
SHEFFIELD S10 2BP

101 775 666 X

D1382125

FAMILY MEDIATION

Past, Present and Future

ONE WEEK LOAN

3 0 SEP 2005

− 8 MAR 2006

− 9 MAR 2006

− 6 MAY 2010

Sheffield Hallam University
Learning and Information Services
Withdrawn From Stock

FAMILY MEDIATION

Past, Present and Future

General Editor
John Westcott

Family Law
2004

Published by
Jordan Publishing Limited
21 St Thomas Street
Bristol BS1 6JS

© Jordan Publishing Limited 2004

All rights reserved. No part of this publication may be reproduced, stored in a retrieval
system, or transmitted in any way or by any means, including photocopying or recording,
without the written permission of the copyright holder, application for which should be
addressed to the publisher.

British Library Cataloguing-in-Publication Data
A catalogue record for this book is available from the British Library.

ISBN 0 85308 948 5

Typeset by Jordan Publishing Limited
Printed in Great Britain by MPG Books Limited, Bodmin, Cornwall

DEDICATION

This book is dedicated to the memory of Janet Forbes

FOREWORD

The Rt Hon Baroness Hale of Richmond

'If only I could bang their heads together . . . .'

Most family judges must at some time or other have had this unworthy feeling when called upon to resolve some apparently petty parental dispute. I well remember having to decide whether two little girls should travel down to London from the far north of England to visit their father for the half-term break on the Friday evening after school (which would be more convenient for him) or on the Saturday morning (which would be less exhausting for them). That issue was easily resolved but I would never be able to resolve the much deeper reasons why it had come my way in the first place.

That is why Gwynn Davis is quite right to say that 'when it comes to disputes about children, judges have no confidence in their own product' (p 63). Court orders are a blunt instrument for resolving the subtle and shifting combinations of practical and emotional problems involved. They are only a little better than banging heads together – a short sharp shock but unlikely to produce lasting relief for anyone, including the judge, who will probably see the same case back again time after time.

Twenty-five years ago it was revolutionary for those in the courts and the legal profession to think that there might be a better way of doing things. No doubt the parents had been thinking so for years. In general, their level of satisfaction with home-made solutions is much higher than with court-imposed ones. We also know now from an ONS Omnibus Survey that 90 per cent of separated parents do not make applications for court orders about their children. They have made arrangements with which they are happy enough not to want to go to court. Not all of these will have been conflict-free. Some of them will have had professional help, from lawyers or others. About 5 per cent of them make use of mediation services.

But the focus of debate and policy-making is still mainly on those cases which would otherwise have to be resolved by a court. It has all become intensely political – not always with a small 'p'. Fathers complain that the courts are biased against them; mothers complain that the courts are obsessed with securing contact no matter what. All are agreed that a lengthy and expensive court process which fails to identify and grapple with the real issues until it is too late is a large part of the problem. So there is general enthusiasm amongst policy-makers and courts for promoting early interventions and alternative methods of resolving matters.

There are many such alternatives including: traditional negotiation between solicitors; the new idea of 'collaborative law' where parties and their solicitors negotiate together on the understanding that the solicitors will not be involved if the case goes to court; information and assistance from a statutory agency associated with the court; and information and assistance from the many independent mediators and mediation services which have followed the Bristol pioneers. Too often these have been seen as rivals rather than complementary services each of which may be able to play a part for a particular family at a particular time.

The 25 years chronicled in this book began with the struggle to get these ideas accepted and the mediation service off the ground. The struggle has continued for most of that time and the future is by no means clear. Over the years Government policy has shifted from tolerant incomprehension of what 'you nice charitable ladies' were trying to do (see p 42) had to do with them; to support for 'quick fix' in-court conciliation whether by welfare officers or district judges; to apparent enthusiasm for independent mediation in the vain hope of stemming the ever-expanding demand for legal aid in family cases, reaching its high point under Part III of the Family Law Act 1996; and now towards a more comprehensive and structured approach to 'family resolutions' involving information, group meetings to explain the problems and possible solutions, and parent planning sessions for both parents to make a parenting plan: the Government's green paper, *Parental Separation: Children's Needs and Parents' Responsibilities* (Cm 6273, July 2004) was published after this book had gone to press. The proposed expansion of in-court conciliation and development of the new approach will mean a large-scale refocusing of the efforts of CAFCASS – away from writing reports for the courts and towards facilitating solutions in this way. This cannot happen unless the courts stop asking for so many reports. One way or another there ought to be plenty of opportunities for mediation services to contribute to the new arrangements.

The Government 'also intends to continue to promote mediation' and proposes to review the relevant rules and Practice Directions so that the strongest possible encouragement is given to parties to agree to mediation or other forms of dispute resolution, in order to ensure that all alternative means of resolving family disputes, short of contested court hearings, are fully utilised' (*Parental Separation*, para 65).

The concept and value of mediation is now widely accepted. It has spread from the family courts to become a recognised part of the civil justice system. The practice of mediation, which began in the touching way described by Kay Begg (p 81), rapidly developed into a highly professional skill with its own standards and values. This has been a remarkable achievement for the Bristol pioneers and the others who followed in their footsteps. This book shows just how much they have to be proud of.

As an unashamed member of the family mediation 'movement' from the early days, and now Chancellor of the University of Bristol, I too am proud to bask in the reflected glory of what began at a meeting at the University all those years ago. Many happy returns!

Brenda Hale
September 2004

CONTENTS

BIOGRAPHIES

John Westcott is Chairman of Bristol Family Mediation and has been a Trustee since 1982. A family lawyer, now retired, he is a former member of the Law Society's Family Law Committee and fellow of the International Academy of Matrimonial Lawyers. A member of the Lord Chancellor's Advisory Committee to the Newcastle University Conciliation Inquiry 1989. He trained and practised as a lawyer mediator with the Family Mediators Association and is a past President of Bristol Law Society.

Dr Stephen Cretney became an academic lawyer in 1965 after a period of practice as a solicitor in the City of London, and held academic appointments in Kenya, Southampton, Bristol and Oxford. He was a Law Commissioner from 1978–1983. He has served as Chairman of Social Security and other tribunals and has been a member of a number of official committees dealing with the prison system, the administration of Family Law, judicial training and legal education. Amongst his publications are *Principles of Family Law* (now in its 7th edition (Sweet & Maxwell, 2002) and jointly edited), *Law, Law Reform and the Family* (OUP, 1998) and *Family Law in the Twentieth Century: A History* (OUP, 2003; paperback edition forthcoming). He is Queen's Counsel *honoris causa*, a Fellow of the British Academy, and an Emeritus Fellow of All Souls College, Oxford.

Mervyn Murch is a Professor of Law at the Cardiff Law School. He was formerly a Senior Research Fellow at the University of Bristol where he established a Centre for Socio-Legal Family Studies. He has academic qualifications in law and applied social studies and has been a social work teacher. In a research career of over 30 years, he has directed a number of projects examining the law and practice of divorce, adoption and the representation of children. He is the author of a number of books. He is a member of the President of the Family Division's Inter-disciplinary Committee and International Committee and a Fellow of the Centre of Social Policy at Dartington.

Lisa Parkinson's experience in social work with families led to her commitment to family mediation and involvement in setting up BCFCS. Lisa became BCFCS co-ordinator and conciliator and a founder member of NFCC (now NFM). Lisa and five SFLA solicitors introduced co-mediation on all issues and set up the Family Mediators Association in 1988. Lisa is a family mediator, supervisor and trainer, has written widely on mediation and taken part in conferences in many countries. She is a committee member of the European Forum on Family Mediation and World Mediation Forum and in 2003 chaired the Scientific Committee at the WMF Conference in Buenos Aires, with participants from 46 countries.

David Woodward was admitted as a solicitor in 1975 and is currently family law partner and head of private business group at TLT Solicitors in Bristol. Past secretary to the then Bristol Courts Conciliation Service. Past chairman of Bristol SFLA. Member of UK College of Mediators. Director of Bristol Family Mediators

Service Limited. Member of Accreditation Committee of the National SFLA. Member of the Law Society Family Law Committee.

Roger Bird is a District Judge at Bristol County Court and High Court District Registry. He was a member of the Children Act Advisory Committee for 6 years and since 1992 has been a member of the Lord Chancellor's (now the President's) Ancillary Relief Advisory Group. He is a former President of the Association of District Judges. He is the author of several books on family law topics. He was a trustee of BFMS before its incorporation and was subsequently an original member of the company.

Gwynn Davis was employed by Bristol University from 1976 until 2001, latterly as Professor of Socio-Legal Studies. He spent most of this time conducting externally funded research projects of a socio-legal character. Many of these concerned the practice of private family law, including mediation, but he was also interested in criminal justice and in developments in the legal profession. He is the author of a number books and articles including *Partisans and Mediators* (OUP, 1988), *Grounds for Divorce* (with M Murch, OUP, 1988), *Simple Quarrels* (with SM Cretney and J Collins, OUP, 1994) and *Child Support in Action* (with N Wikeley and R Young, Hart Publishing, 1998). He remains attached to Bristol Law School as Honorary Senior Research Fellow.

Thelma Fisher's career began in social work, social work education and marital counselling. She became the co-ordinator/mediator of the Swindon Family Conciliation Service in 1981 before returning to teach at the University of Bath. In 1989 she became the first Director of National Family Mediation, developing the provision and standards of mediation in the not-for-profit sector. She represented mediation during the Family Law Bill in 1996 and from 1999–2003 was the Chair of the UK College of Family Mediators. She has edited two books on family mediation and written two consumer guides, the latest *Divorce for Dummies* with Hilary Woodward, a family lawyer who mediates with the Bristol Family Mediation Service.

Kay Begg was a mediator and supervisor for 25 years and helped set up, establish and manage Bristol Family Mediation. She was Vice-Chairman of National Family Mediation for 6 years, acting as Chairman on three occasions. During this time, she played an active part in forming family mediation standards and practice, and in 1996 she became a Governor of the UK College of Family Mediators and its first Vice-Chairman. In 2000 she was awarded an OBE for services to family mediation. She retired as a practising mediator in 2002.

Trevor Morkham After graduating in law in 1972, Trevor went on to complete his social work training (CQSW) and then entered the Probation Service. A brief spell in research was followed by 10 years as a social worker with Child and Family Guidance in Wiltshire, where an abiding interest in Family Therapy was kindled and nurtured. In 1984, he joined the Family Mediation Service in Swindon as a sessional mediator, going on to become full-time manager of Bristol Family Mediation in 1990. Throughout his 12 years as manager, Trevor continued practising as a mediator alongside his managerial responsibilities and the decision to step down from the managerial role in 2002 was prompted in part by the desire to concentrate more on the practice side. He is currently Practice Manager with the North Wiltshire (formerly Swindon) Family Mediation Service and also supervises mediators for both BFM and for NCH Cymru Family Mediation in Newport in his capacity as Professional Practice Consultant (PPC) for those services.

Elizabeth Walsh Elizabeth Walsh is editor of Family Law and International Family Law. She is also a practising family mediator, a chairman of the family proceedings court and from 1997–1999 was Chief Executive of the UK College of Family Mediators. In 1997 she wrote a book on interdisciplinary co-operation for the National Council for Family Proceedings: *Working in the Family Justice System* (Jordans).

Introduction

THE ORIGINS AND DEVELOPMENT OF FAMILY MEDIATION IN THE UK

John Westcott

This year Bristol Family Mediation celebrates the 25th anniversary of its launch, in 1979, as the Bristol Courts Family Conciliation Service, the first local family conciliation service in the UK. In the intervening years family mediation, as it is now called, has developed in several different forms and has become an established part of the family justice system. Looking back over those years (still somewhat incredulous that we have managed to survive that long) and to mark our anniversary, we decided that we should compile an account of the origins of the family mediation, from the perspective of those who were closely involved, as well as of the development of the family mediation movement generally, incorporating our own history.

Inevitably with a pioneering venture, seen by many during the early years as not much more than a voluntary and local piece of social work, we encountered a succession of problems, not least in the search for adequate and regular funding. As other local services, such as ours, began to be set up in other parts of the country, other issues, such as the working out and establishing generally accepted principles of practice nationally, became central and influential in the wider development of family mediation.

We have been fortunate enough to assemble a team of distinguished contributors, who have either been closely associated with a particular, and usually problematic, period in Bristol's history, or have been involved in one of the more general issues that I have referred to. Each was given a free hand to make whatever comment he or she felt was appropriate.

The reader will soon realise that the history of mediation has not been entirely free from controversy. In a movement whose *raison d'être* is conflict resolution, one's first thought might be that disagreement should be avoided but I think it is fair to say that occasional differences of opinion, sensibly managed, have had positive results. Certainly, the new discourse between lawyers and sociologists that family mediation has generated has been both intriguing and constructive. In the sense that useful lessons can always be learned from the past, our hope (expressed by Elizabeth Walsh in the final chapter) is that this book might make a contribution to the future and further development of family mediation.

We could hardly have started this book in a better way than with a first chapter from Dr Stephen Cretney, recently described as the doyen of family lawyers. He shows how the attitude of the courts towards marital breakdown has changed since the beginning of the twenty-first century. From the preservation of the institution of marriage as the primary objective, the huge increase in divorce post-war forced attention to be directed to the social consequences of divorce. So it was that stratagems to achieve reconciliation and so save marriages began to be replaced by conciliation as a way of helping spouses to find solutions to the problems their separation was producing. It was this concept of conciliation which the Finer Committee in 1974 articulated. When the basis of mediation now is to encourage separating spouses to discuss their problems together, it is salutary to be reminded by Dr Cretney that it was not so long ago that any collusion between spouses was an absolute bar to their getting a divorce.

The traditional view that divorce law should protect the institution of marriage 'as a force for good in society as a whole'[1] was of very long standing, but, in 1966, the Law Commission moved somewhat away from that position defining the objectives of a good divorce law as *not only* (1) to buttress rather than undermine the stability of marriage *but also* (2) when marriage had irretrievably broken down, to enable the legal shell to be destroyed with the maximum fairness and minimum bitterness.[2] Nearly 30 years later, in 1995, Lord Mackay, when he was Lord Chancellor and was introducing his government's proposals for reforming divorce law, still felt able to comment 'that marriage should be for life (as providing) the most stable background for the birth and development of children'.[3]

Nevertheless, as several of our contributors have observed, there was a rapid rise in the divorce rate in England in the 1970s. In 1987 it was predicted that nearly one-third of marriages would end in divorce within 20 years.[4] It became apparent that our substantive divorce law was proving to be unsuccessful in achieving the declared primary objective of stabilising or protecting marriage.

When primary legislation, intended to improve the substantive divorce law, has come before Parliament, as it did again in 1996, the ensuing debate has inevitably illustrated the difficulty in reconciling in legislation the desire to support the institution of marriage at the same time as making the divorce process less contentious, without necessarily making divorce easier. The result was the compromise of the Family Law Act of that year with Part II of that Act, which would have allowed a marriage to be dissolved after a period of separation and which would have been the most significant change in the law, never being implemented.

More effective progress has been made in pursuing the Law Commission's second objective, through the device of procedural change rather than by primary legislation. Dr Cretney has observed elsewhere:

---

[1]   G Davis and M Murch *Grounds for Divorce* (1988).
[2]   Law Commission *The Field of Choice* (1966) Cmnd 3123.
[3]   HMSO *Looking to the Future* (1995) Cmnd 2799.
[4]   K Kiernan and M Wicks *Family Change and Future Policy* (1990).

'It could be argued that, in relation to divorce, procedural change has, over the years, had more impact than changes in the substantive law.'[1]

Through such change, the divorce process became less adversarial and more inquisitorial. Changes in court procedure removed the need for petitioners to go into court to prove irretrievable breakdown or to satisfy judges personally about the arrangements being made for their children.

If it was the shift in emphasis onto the consequences of divorce and therefore upon the divorce process which germinated the concept of conciliation, it was given further impetus by an increasing unhappiness on the part of the divorcing public with what was still an adversarial process, and which many thought introduced an unnecessary element of conflict. Divorce lawyers, who were obliged to advise their clients to be separately represented, came under attack for fomenting conflict in order to increase their fees. In dealing with the problems which inevitably followed separation, especially deciding on the future of the children and the division of family assets, most people accepted that they had a mutual interest in finding solutions and they wanted to find a way of doing this as amicably as possible.

Professor Murch, in his chapter, observes that the 1974 Finer Report, introducing the concept of conciliation, emphasised the importance of separating parties retaining some control over the solving of the issues which their separation had produced rather than decisions being made for them by the court. It was following Professor Murch's research into the impact of divorce on families, and influenced by Finer, that a conference of local legal and social work practitioners and academics in Bristol proposed the setting up of a local and experimental conciliation service. As he says, it was a formidable challenge and he gives an account of the many problems which had to be overcome initially, some of which continued to worry the eventual new service for some considerable time.

Lisa Parkinson was the first Co-ordinator of Bristol Courts Family Conciliation Service when it was formally launched in 1979 and, in her chapter, she describes the problems which she had to deal with leading up to that launch and in the early years. She shows how the principles of family conciliation (later to be called mediation) were worked out and became accepted nationally, forming the basis of what eventually became the widely successful mediation movement.

At the same time as these moves were taking place outside the court system, the senior registrar (as district judges were then called) in Bristol County Court, Geoffrey Parmiter, was pioneering a system of court directions in family matters which persuaded parties away from conflict in favour of conciliation, either with a court welfare officer or by referral to the new, out of court, BCFCS. This initiative had the effect of reducing the number of contested divorce proceedings and was helpful in giving, as it were, official approval to conciliation as an alternative to contested proceedings.

---

[1] S Cretney *Family Law in the Twentieth Century: A History* (OUP, 2003), at p 165.

Obtaining adequate and regular funding was a major problem for the new BCFCS. At the outset it was felt that, if the service could be accepted as not just a voluntary alternative to court proceedings but as an established part of the family justice system, government funding would have to follow. In 1982, as we faced yet another financial crisis, Lord Waldegrave, then a Bristol MP, and one of our first patrons, who actively supported our project, arranged an interview with Lord Hailsham, then Lord Chancellor, in the hope that he might be able to produce some government funding for us.

I had just become a trustee and was asked to present our case to him. As my usual stamping ground was the local county court, appearing before the Lord Chancellor was a new experience but, soon after I had begun speaking, I got the not unfamiliar feeling that his lordship was not with me. Further embarrassment was saved by the division bell summoning him to House of Lords chamber. As he left Lord Hailsham said that he thought it fairly unlikely that the Treasury could be persuaded to find any money for us and that we would do well to go back to Bristol and hold a few coffee mornings to raise the money we needed.

We came away realising that we would have to do a great deal more to persuade those in authority that what we were about was not just a limited and local exercise in voluntary social work by some 'charitable ladies' (an early comment which Lisa Parkinson recalls in her chapter). In fairness, when I met Lord Hailsham a few years later at a social function in Bristol, he had clearly informed himself about our work and was more encouraging. Also during the year (1983) in which the first of the government inquiries into conciliation was deliberating, we were funded by the Lord Chancellor's Department whilst that inquiry's conclusions were awaited.

It is perhaps as well that we had no means of knowing then that it was going to take us another 15 years for Bristol to get its first regular government funding by way of a legal aid contract. During those ensuing years, we were entirely dependent on the untiring and effective efforts of fund raisers, first Christine Porter and, later, Julie Axford. They succeeded in getting us grants from a number of local and national charities. These included the first grant from the Van Neste Foundation, then the Society of Merchant Venturers, the Tudor Trust, the Greater Bristol Foundation, Portishead Nautical Trust, and many others. For several years, the salary of our service manager was paid by Avon Probation Service. Even so, I can recall no less than five occasions when our money almost ran out and we had to ensure that we had enough left in the bank to make staff redundancy payments.

The primary objective, in those early years, was to show that we were offering a genuine and responsible alternative to contested divorce proceedings in the court. To that end, it was important that the service be staffed by trained people, experienced in family matters and in whom divorcing or separating spouses could place their confidence.

Therefore, the response of the general public to this new initiative was crucial and, as Lisa Parkinson shows, that response was positive and immediate. By the end of the first 6 months, 50 active cases were being dealt with. Inevitably there were critics. Some believed that a service which concentrated on the consequences of separation would make divorce easier. Some local solicitors were apprehensive, and some were openly hostile, being anxious to retain work with divorcing couples which, after all, had been the sole preserve of lawyers since the reign of Henry VIII.

Soon the professional quality of the work of the conciliators and the results they were producing, as David Woodward explains in his chapter, began to persuade solicitors that conciliation could be complementary to the legal issues which it was still necessary for lawyers to deal with. Local solicitors began to refer clients to the service and it was not long before Bristol Law Society was financially helping the new service. With the advent of the Family Mediators Association in 1988, lawyers began to be trained as lawyer mediators and family mediation is now offered by many law firms.

The growth of a more conciliatory attitude on the part of practising lawyers was also encouraged by the further evolution in Bristol County Court, which District Judge Roger Bird describes in his chapter, of the pragmatic style introduced by Mr Registrar Parmiter. Even after court proceedings had been commenced, parties were invited to consider the alternative of mediation, and, if the response was favourable, were referred by the court either to a court welfare officer or to our service.

In order to persuade those in authority that the mediation alternative was capable of becoming permanent, independent evaluation was going to be essential. We were fortunate that, at an early stage, Professor Gwynn Davis researched the work we were doing critically and, most importantly, interviewed clients who had consulted our service. He has probably done more research into the different aspects of mediation than anyone else so the observations in his chapter are particularly valuable. He it was who poured cold water on the early notion some of us had that the best way to get support for conciliation was to claim that it was bound to be cheaper than contested proceedings in court. He shows how rather better measures of value have subsequently emerged.

Establishing credibility also depended on demonstrating that our mediators were not only trained and properly accredited but followed a laid down common code of practice. As more services were set up so the need arose for a national umbrella body who would control the training and accreditation of mediators and monitor the code of practice. Thelma Fisher, in her chapter, describes how the National Conciliation Council (later to become National Family Mediation) came into being. She also makes the interesting observation that conciliation may well have been a feature of society's need to adjust to the post-modern rapid social change of the 1970s.

Fundamental developments in the Bristol service took place during the time (from 1990–2002) when Trevor Morkham was the service manager. By the end of his tenure, as he recounts in his chapter, the service eventually achieved financial stability but not before Trevor had to survive one year when Avon Probation

Service was obliged to withdraw its funding of his salary. In the financial year of 2003, for the very first time, our annual income matched our annual expenditure. In 1997, Bristol obtained its first contract with the Legal Aid Board (LAB); the long-awaited government funding; but it was not the end of our problems.

The concept of a 'not-for-profit' service, as we were, seemed simple enough to us. We budget simply to cover our regular expenditure with regular income. It follows that if there is any delay in getting contracted income we immediately encounter a cash-flow problem and have to draw on our reserves. For some reason this fact was not immediately apparent to our new funders and, in 1999, because of delayed payments under the LAB contract, we had to weather yet another financial crisis. Subsequently these contracts, now with the Legal Services Commission, have been renewed annually without further difficulty and by the time this book is published new contracts with standard arrangements for all not-for-profit services will have been introduced.

In 1997 the Bristol service also became incorporated, as a private company limited by guarantee and so achieved the metamorphosis from an experimental project, perceived initially as a local voluntary effort, into an established service of proven viability. Perhaps it is inevitable that professionals should adopt a rather patronising attitude initially towards any voluntary effort but I believe that we have succeeded in showing that the voluntary ethos, which can generate a new idea, can also make it work in a professional manner.

Because of all the different issues with which we and other family mediation providers have struggled over the years: funding, accreditation, working with lawyers and the courts, and so on, it is easy to forget that the fundamental reason why mediation has become established and accepted is, quite simply, the high quality and professionalism of the work done by family mediators which soon became recognised by judges, lawyers and social workers and, most importantly, by the general public. Their largely unsung work runs like a golden thread through all the years of Bristol's history and of the family mediation movement generally.

Kay Begg, who has the distinction of being one of Bristol's very first conciliators and who has remained with us ever since, now as a director and mediator supervisor, describes in her chapter how the role of the family mediator has developed during that time; quite recently into new fields and also how, over the years, family mediators have accumulated a wide and unique knowledge of what Professor Murch calls 'the psychodynamics of family life'.

As we look back over the past 25 years, those involved in the family mediation movement can feel justified in claiming that a countless number of people throughout the United Kingdom will have been helped sympathetically through the painful process of family breakdown. The venture that started in Bristol all those years ago and which has now spread throughout the country and been taken up in a variety of different ways has, one ventures to hope, gone some way in achieving the second objective of the 1966 Law Commission in minimising the bitterness and the hurt of separation for many people and their children.

We asked Elizabeth Walsh who, as editor of *Family Law*, has her finger on the pulse of family law, as well as practical experience as a family mediator, to end this book with some thoughts on the likely future of family mediation. Arguing for a holistic approach, she examines critically what seem like a recent plethora of reports and new initiatives in the field of the family within a general acceleration of alternative dispute resolution into many new areas.

Yet it is apparent from what she says that some of the issues which have exercised our minds from the outset still remain unresolved. For instance, whilst many in the mediation movement have considered the concepts of mediation and compulsion to be mutually exclusive, both Liz Walsh and, interestingly Roger Bird, suggest that mediation may have to become compulsory. I still have a letter sent to me 20 years ago by Professor Frank Sander of Harvard Law School in which he expressed the view that he would have no trouble with an element of coercion into mediation but that any coercion within the process of mediation should be unacceptable. So whilst this book is, on one level, an account of problems and difficulties successfully overcome, it also identifies a number of issues which family mediators must still tackle. It seems likely that the next few years may be no more comfortable than the last 25.

Chapter 1

CONCILIATION, RECONCILIATION AND MEDIATION: THE HISTORICAL CONTEXT

Dr Stephen Cretney

Introduction: the courts and the family

At the beginning of the twenty-first century, litigation about the consequences of family relationships is usually associated with proceedings in the Family Division of the High Court or in the county court. But this was not always so. A century ago it was the magistrates' courts (administering the system of family justice originally created[1] primarily to protect wives from domestic violence) which had the most experience of dealing with domestic problems: they made orders in 5,000 or so cases each year at a time when the divorce court granted a mere 500 or so decrees, and the number of court *orders* made did not necessarily reflect the number of *applications* to the magistrates. In 1922 Sir Chartres Biron, the Chief Metropolitan Magistrate, told a Parliamentary Select Committee[2] that his objective was:

> 'to keep people out of court if possible. You cannot expect an ideal home in Hoxton any more than perhaps you can in Mayfair, but you want to get the thing on a reasonable basis, and what we always tried to do was to get the people together if possible. Before granting any summons I always went very carefully into the cases and a great many were obviously frivolous applications ... The whole object in all these matters dealing with women and children and husbands was at all costs, even at some sacrifice of the individual, to keep the homes together, because we were always firmly persuaded that it was very much better for people to live together even under circumstances of some discomfort and with occasional outbreaks ...'

This passage highlights many issues which remained controversial for much of the twentieth century. For example: how far should the law restrict the right of immediate access to the courts – whether by refusing to grant a woman's 'frivolous' application for protection against a husband who was perhaps 'no worse than many', or even by requiring attendance at an 'information' meeting as a preliminary to starting divorce proceedings? And what is the function of a court hearing cases based on relationship breakdown: is it to 'keep the home together' or to 'save the marriage'?[3] How far should it be for the court itself to seek to 'conciliate'? What arrangements should be made for counselling and other help?

---

[1] The most important statute was the Summary Jurisdiction (Married Women) Act 1895.

[2] *Joint Select Committee on the Guardianship of Infants Bill, Minutes of Evidence*, 19 July 1922, q.9.

[3] See Family Law Act 1996, s 1(b). The same Act, in provisions which are not to be brought into force, stipulated that those contemplating divorce should attend an 'information meeting' not less than 3 months before starting proceedings, and that there should thereafter be a period for 'reflection and consideration' before a divorce or separation order could be made: ss 8, 9.

'Conciliation' in domestic cases

There was certainly a great diversity of practice between different magistrates' courts. In some areas, the main burden of 'conciliation' fell on the Police Court Missionaries (some working for the Church of England Temperance Society, others for the Salvation Army); and other courts relied on independent volunteers (such as the Chelsea doctor's wife with a 'superior education' who worked at the Thames court). But the Probation of Offenders Act 1907 marked the beginning of the involvement of trained probation officers discharging what had become a statutory role of 'advising and befriending' those involved with the legal system. In many courts, the justices' clerk was active, especially in emphasising the economic costs of separation and urging those tempted to seek a court order to think again. And in some quarters[1] there was strong support for involving the magistrates themselves in 'conciliation' at least to the extent of training them in the causes of marital disharmony and encouraging them to refer cases to the missionary or probation officer.

By 1934 the Lord Chancellor could tell Parliament[2] that in one way or another it was often possible to bring couples – often young people whose quarrel was due to inexperience and ignorance – 'to a better frame of mind and to guide them to a settlement. In such cases and in many others it is possible for a mediator of experience to remove misunderstandings, to show how difficulties may be overcome and to bring about a permanent reconciliation ...'. In 1936 the Departmental Committee on the Social Services in Courts of Summary Jurisdiction[3] advocated the provision of 'machinery for conciliation' (a facility in general to be provided by the Probation Service) in the magistrates' courts; and by the end of the Second World War it could be said[4] that in all 'properly conducted' magistrates' courts a probation officer would 'have a shot at effecting conciliation'; and that adjournment for reconciliation was 'the common practice' in the magistrates' courts and 'often achieved its object'.[5] The magistrates were only to be involved in the process of 'conciliation' to this limited extent. Their business

---

[1]   Claud Mullins, the Metropolitan Police Magistrate at the South-West London court, played a leading role: see generally GK Behlmer *Friends of the Family, The English Home and its Guardians, 1850–1940* (1998). Mullins was responsible for persuading the young Labour Peer, Lord Listowel, to bring a Summary Jurisdiction (Domestic Procedure) Bill into the House of Lords in 1934; and, although that Bill did not make progress, the debate on its second reading influenced the Government's decision to extend the terms of reference of the Departmental Committee on the Social Services in Courts of Summary Jurisdiction to the procedure and constitution of magistrates' domestic courts. The Committee's *Report* Cmnd 5122 (1936) was influential in the development of the concept of conciliation and its application in the context of court proceedings: see below.

[2]   In the debate on the Summary Jurisdiction (Domestic Procedure) Bill introduced by Lord Listowel: *Official Report (HL)*, 15 May 1934, vol 92, col 382 (Lord Sankey).

[3]   Cmnd 5122, para 13.

[4]   By Lord Merriman (President of the Probate Divorce and Admiralty Division from 1933 until his death, aged 82, in 1966) giving evidence to the (Denning) *Committee on Procedure in Matrimonial Causes*.

[5]   For research concluding that in the inter-war years conciliators were often successful in persuading applicants to cease legal action see G Behlmer, 'Summary Justice and Working-Class Marriage in England, 1870–1940' (1994) 12 Law and History Review 229, at 238 and generally GK Behlmer, *Friends of the Family, The English Home and its Guardians, 1850–1940* (1998), pp 213–229 ('Claud Mullins and Coercive Conciliation').

was adjudication: they needed to have an awareness of the social implications of marriage breakdown and a knowledge of the 'facilities for conciliation' available to those coming to the court, but it was not a proper function of a court of law to seek to give the parties advice or counselling.[1] It seems clear that 'conciliation' at this time was directed to bringing husband and wife together (although if this was not achieved the probation officer might clarify the issues between them so that the magistrates could themselves help the parties to put their case).[2]

'Conciliation' in divorce

At this period, 'conciliation' did not seem to be a live issue in divorce proceedings. In part, this may have been because divorce, founded exclusively on proof of the commission of a matrimonial offence,[3] involved a considerable social stigma[4] and so cases in which there was the remotest prospect of reconciliation did not reach the Divorce Court.[5] In part it may have been because an important function of the Divorce Court was to prevent people escaping from the legal status of marriage by private agreement[6] and to enforce the policy that divorce by consent remains 'remote from the contemplation of English law'. For this reason, 'collusion' was an absolute bar to divorce; and in practice lawyers routinely advised 'matrimonial' clients to have nothing to do with one another – not even to discuss the arrangements necessary to deal with housing, money and children for fear that to do so might debar them from the divorce which they had come to recognise as the appropriate legal solution for the breakdown of their marriage.[7]

Changing attitudes

Divorce for long remained a minority pursuit: until World War I, divorce petitions could be counted in hundreds rather than thousands. The main function of the divorce judges was to decide the conceptually simple question of whether the admissible evidence showed that the respondent had indeed committed the adultery which the petition alleged. This seemed, and indeed was, a perfectly justiciable issue. But by the end of the Second World War things were different in a number of respects. A long campaign for divorce law reform had achieved its main

---

[1] The *Report of the Departmental Committee on the Social Services in Courts of Summary Jurisdiction* Cmnd 5122 (1936) ('the Harris Report') established this as the orthodox view. For an account of the attempts to allocate a substantial role to the court itself, see SM Cretney, *Family Law in the Twentieth Century: A History* (OUP, 2003), pp 290–298.

[2] See Summary Jurisdiction (Domestic Proceedings) Act 1937, ss 4–6.

[3] The Matrimonial Causes Act 1937 had extended the grounds for divorce to include cruelty and desertion.

[4] For example, the divorced were excluded from Royal Garden Parties and from the Royal Enclosure at Ascot; and the divorced were unlikely to be regarded as suitable candidates for judicial appointment: see PRO LCO 2/4618, 11 July 1947. At the same period, a diplomat with a distinguished record of service (eg as Chairman of the Joint Intelligence Committee during the Second World War) was summarily dismissed and forfeited his substantial pension rights because divorce proceedings revealed that he had committed adultery: see P Howarth *Intelligence Chief Extraordinary, The Life of the Ninth Duke of Portland* (Bodley Head, 1986).

[5] Committee on Procedure in Matrimonial Causes Final Report Cmnd 7024 (1947), para10.

[6] See SM Cretney, *Family Law in the Twentieth Century: A History* (OUP, 2003), at p 177ff.

[7] See *Report of the Royal Commission on Marriage and Divorce* Cmnd 8130 (1956) (subsequently 'the Morton Report') para 231.

objectives in 1937: cruelty and desertion were added to the grounds for divorce thereby greatly broadening the range of issues to be decided by the divorce judges, and a decision of the House of Lords in 1943 had significantly eroded the principle that divorce was only to be available to those innocent of any matrimonial offence. Divorce became legally possible for many denied this relief in the past. This, combined with the devastating impact of war-time conditions on family life in general and marriage in particular, was a factor in the huge increase in the number of divorce petitions in the immediate post-war period. The court system was threatened with breakdown: it was said that scenes outside some courts were 'more reminiscent of Epsom Downs than a court of justice'.[1] But it was not only respect for the legal system which was threatened. The Archbishop of Canterbury and the Lord Chancellor were not alone in believing that the increase in demand for divorce threatened the whole idea of Christian marriage.[2]

Something clearly had to be done. The Government set up a Committee chaired by Mr Justice Denning[3] to recommend reform of divorce *procedure* (the *ground* for divorce was specifically excluded from the committee's remit) and also to consider 'in particular whether any (and if so what) machinery should be made available for the purpose of attempting a reconciliation between the parties, whether before or after proceedings have been commenced'. The Committee found a solution to the immediate problem of overload on the courts by recommending that all the county court judges, dressed up (and paid) for the day as High Court judges, should be appointed as Commissioners to try divorce cases. In this way (so the Committee opined)[4] the 'careful and dignified' High Court procedure would encourage a 'respectful view of the marriage tie and status'.

But what of conciliation? Here the Committee did not start with a blank piece of paper: the President, Lord Merriman, had already put forward a scheme under which all undefended divorce cases would be referred to a statutory Commission of Conciliation and Enquiry made up of a lawyer and welfare worker or probation officer. It would be for the Commission to explore the possibilities of effecting a reconciliation between the parties. Only if there were no reconciliation would the tribunal deal with financial and custody issues, remitting the case to the court to grant the divorce decree. Merriman's proposal was supported by all the Divorce judges, by the Archbishops of York and Canterbury, and by Lord Chancellor Jowitt. But the Denning Committee[5] rejected the President's scheme out of hand. It gave two reasons. First, reconciliation had to be attempted 'long before proceedings were begun' if there were to be any prospects of success.[6] Secondly,

---

[1]   Second Interim Report of the Committee on Procedure in Matrimonial Causes Cmnd 6945 (1946), para 6(1).

[2]   See SM Cretney *Law, Law Reform and the Family* (OUP, 1998), pp 138–139, notes 8 and 12.

[3]   It is often forgotten that Denning was first appointed to the High Court bench in 1943 as a judge of the Probate Divorce and Admiralty Division. In 1945 (as was the common practice until, perhaps, as recently as the 1990s) he was transferred to more congenial duties in the Queen's Bench Division.

[4]   Second Interim Report of the Committee on Procedure in Matrimonial Causes Cmnd 6945 (1946), para 4.

[5]   Final Report of the Committee on Procedure in Matrimonial Causes Cmnd 7024 (1947).

[6]   Ibid, para 25.

the Committee – adopting much the same reasoning as the 1936 Harris Committee – believed there should be a sharp distinction between the judicial role on the one hand and the essentially social work task of providing treatment (and hopefully cures) for marriages which seemed to have failed on the other. Hence, whilst there should be a State-sponsored (but not State-run) 'Marriage Welfare Service' to give 'help and guidance', this should function quite separately from the judicial procedure for divorce.[1] A measure of funding for marriage guidance and welfare services was made available;[2] and a decade later the Royal Commission on Marriage and Divorce[3] supported expanded provision of skilled counselling to help husband and wife 'overcome their difficulties' and to achieve a reconciliation.[4] The Royal Commission recommended improved State financial support for agencies engaged in matrimonial 'conciliation',[5] and the expansion of what was to become the divorce court welfare service.

The Divorce Reform Act 1969: ending marriage a matter for the parties

By the beginning of the 1960s, there seemed to be general agreement that the courts had no direct function in 'conciliation' and that the overriding objective of 'conciliation' was to save the marriage. But how far were these principles affected by the Divorce Reform Act 1969? The long title to the Act described it as 'an Act to amend the grounds for divorce and judicial separation and to facilitate reconciliation': s 1 of the Act provided that the 'sole ground' for divorce was to be that the marriage had 'broken down irretrievably'; whilst s 3 contained a number of specific 'provisions designed to encourage reconciliation' (including what might appear to be a requirement for the petitioner's solicitor to discuss reconciliation and to direct the petitioner to a reconciliation agency, as well as a specific power for the court to adjourn proceedings to enable attempts to be made to effect a reconciliation). Neither of these provisions meant what they seemed to say. In reality, the Act *required* the court to grant the divorce provided that the petitioner could establish that the respondent had been guilty of adultery, cruelty or desertion – the Act used slightly different language but the underlying concepts were identical to those familiar in the divorce court for more than a century – or that there had been a separation for a stipulated period the length of which differed according to whether the parties were agreed on divorce or not. So far as reconciliation was concerned, the Act did *not* require the petitioner's solicitor actually to discuss reconciliation, but merely to certify *whether* or not he had done so. In case there should be any doubt about what was to happen, a *Practice Direction*[6] emphasised that reference to a marriage guidance counsellor or probation officer should not be regarded as a formal step to be undertaken in all cases. On the contrary, there should be no reference unless there was a 'sincere desire for reconciliation'.

---

[1] Final Report of the Committee on Procedure in Matrimonial Causes Cmnd 7024 (1947), para 28(iii).
[2] Departmental Committee on Grants for the Development of Marriage Guidance Cmnd 7566 (1948).
[3] Royal Commission on Marriage and Divorce Cmnd 9678, Part IV (1956).
[4] Morton Report, para 339.
[5] Ibid, para 349.
[6] *Practice Direction (Divorce: Reconciliation) (No 2)* [1972] 1 WLR 1309.

What of the role of the court in all this? Again, there were words[1] in the Act which might have suggested that the court hearing a divorce petition was to carry out a serious and perhaps detailed investigation: it was specifically provided that it was to be the court's duty to 'inquire, so far as it reasonably can, into the facts alleged by the petitioner and into any facts alleged by the respondent. Those words were deliberately chosen to echo earlier legislation designed to prevent collusion;[2] but the Divorce Reform Act 1969[3] had consigned collusion (along with the other bars to divorce) to the dustbin of history: under the new law, the fact that husband and wife had reached agreement was to be a matter for congratulation not censure. It soon became clear that if one of the parties wanted a divorce and the prescribed formalities were observed, sooner or later (and sooner if both parties were agreed) divorce there would be. The courts had ceased to have any meaningful role in determining whether an unhappily married couple should continue to be legally bound together.

Consequences of divorce still a matter for court monitoring

At the same time, the divorce reform package greatly increased the functions of the court in relation to the *consequences* of dissolution. So far as arrangements for the children were concerned, the legislation[4] extended the scope of provisions dating from 1958 which reflected the belief[5] that the court should look into the arrangements to be made for the children's upbringing whether the parties wanted it to do so or not. And the principle that a couple's financial relationships are a matter of vital public interest not to be settled by any private agreement between them[6] remained untouched by legislation which greatly facilitated the making of orders affecting the entirety of the parties' assets and income. So although the reformed divorce legislation might leave the decision whether to end marriage to the parties, it continued to deny them any right definitively to settle the financial and child-related consequences of that decision. The courts might have lost one role, but had quickly been found another.

The 'problem' of divorce and the one-parent family

Whatever else may be said about the impact of the 1969 divorce reforms – and the fact that thousands of men and women, legally bound by the ties of a marriage which had long ceased to function, were given the freedom to marry again which

---

[1]   Divorce Reform Act 1969, s 2(2).
[2]   Matrimonial Causes Act 1857, s 29; Matrimonial Causes Act 1937, s 4. This latter provision was intended to provide a more effective barrier against divorce by mutual consent: see Cretney, *Family Law in the Twentieth Century: A History* (OUP, 2003), at pp 243–245.
[3]   Section 9(2) and Schedule.
[4]   Matrimonial Proceedings and Property Act 1970, s 18. (As part of a compromise, it had been agreed that this Act, containing provisions about children and financial matters, should be brought into force on the same date as the Divorce Reform Act 1969: see Cretney, op cit, at pp 374, 420.)
[5]   The provisions of the Matrimonial Proceedings (Children) Act 1958 reflected the view of the Morton Report (para 366) that it was wrong for divorce to be regarded as simply a matter for the husband and the wife, since this meant that there would be 'no adequate means' of ensuring that someone should be 'specially charged to look after the children's interests'.
[6]   The divorce court thus has a 'paternal role' in protecting the public interest: *Pounds v Pounds* [1994] 1 FLR 775, at 780, per Waite LJ; *Hyman v Hyman* [1929] AC 601, at 614, per Lord Hailsham.

many had long craved is certainly an important consideration – it cannot be argued that the new law reduced the amount of formally recognised marriage breakdown. In 1965 (when there were 42,070 divorce petitions) the Law Commission had forecast that allowing divorce after 5 years' separation might be followed by an increase of some 5,000 in the annual number of divorces. In fact, there were 110,017 divorce petitions in the first year of operation of the Divorce Reform Act, and thereafter the number of petitions never fell below 100,000. The divorce rate in England and Wales became one of the highest in Europe.[1]

Such figures no doubt worried old-fashioned believers in marriage as a life-long union, and they certainly worried a Government which in one way and another bore a significant share of the financial cost. Unlike the moralists, the Government could take action to minimise the damage. Seizing on an impressive piece of research by Mervyn Murch and others (which had demonstrated that judicial hearings of undefended divorce petitions did not appear to serve any useful purpose) the Government introduced – at first on a limited scale – the so-called 'special procedure'. No more was public money to be wasted on judicial hearings to decide whether the court should grant a decree and so legal aid could safely be withdrawn (although legal aid would remain for dealing with financial matters). An elaborate procedure was introduced under which the judiciary were required to scrutinise and assess the child-raising arrangements which the parents had agreed. This opportunity to discuss what was to happen with a judge would (so the Lord Chancellor told the House of Lords[2]) ensure that the law continued to protect children. But once again these expectations were not fulfilled: another research project[3] found the children's appointments system to be largely ineffective; 3 years later a Law Commission Working Paper[4] concluded that it had 'not been successful in any of its declared aims', and the coup de grace was duly administered by the Children Act 1989.[5] Even in accountant's terms, it seems that the special procedure had been a failure: any savings in funding the hearing of petitions were more than outweighed by greatly increased expenditure on funding litigation about money and resolving contests about access and custody.[6]

So there was increasing concern about the effects of marital breakdown. At one level, the belief that allowing divorce for 'irretrievable breakdown' would minimise bitterness and distress did not seem to have been well founded; and it was suggested that adversarial litigation about the *consequences* of the breakdown might be at least a contributory factor in the failure of the 1969 reforms to achieve one of their promoter's most important objectives. But at the same time there was also serious disquiet about the apparent growth in the number of single-parent

[1]   A significant proportion of divorce petitions do not lead to decrees. Even so, the number of decrees rose from some 89,000 in 1971 to peak at 165,018 in 1993; and whereas in 1971 there were six divorces for every thousand married persons, by 1991 the rate had risen to 13.5 per thousand.

[2]   *Official Report (HL)* 15 June 1976, vol 371, col 1218.

[3]   'Undefended Divorce: Should Section 41 of the Matrimonial Causes Act 1973 be Repealed?' G Davis, A MacLeod and M Murch (1983) 46 MLR 121.

[4]   Working Paper No 96, *Review of Child Law: Custody* (1986), para 4.10.

[5]   See Children Act 1989, s 108(4) and Sch 12, para 31.

[6]   See 32nd Annual Report of the Law Society on the Operation and Finance of the Legal Aid Scheme 1981/1982, paras 77–106.

families and the economic and social disadvantages which such families often
suffered. In 1969, the Wilson Government had set up a Committee with the
breathtakingly broad remit of considering 'the problems of one-parent families in
our society'. These problems were by no means exclusively or even primarily
legal, and the (Finer) Committee on One-Parent Families did make detailed
recommendations for a new non-contributory social benefit (the 'Guaranteed
Maintenance Allowance') intended to alleviate the financial problems inevitably
affecting many such families, as well as on child care provision, employment and
housing law and practice. But the emphasis of the Finer Committee's massive
report, published in the summer of 1974, was very much on the impact which the
law had on society, and reflected the distinctive interests and background of the
Committee's Chairman, Sir Morris Finer[1] (a lawyer of left-wing views, who had,
from an underprivileged background, built up a large professional practice in
commercial and financial cases) and his close friend since student days, the social
historian Professor OR McGregor.[2] Unhappily, publication of the Committee's
Report[3] coincided with a period of grave economic difficulty; and most of the
Committee's detailed recommendations fell victim to the overriding need to reduce
public expenditure. But in at least two respects the *Report* had a great and long-
lasting influence for the family justice system. First, the Committee urged the
creation of a system of 'family courts' which would efficiently administer a unified
set of legal rules rather than itself administer therapy. Secondly, the family court
was to be equipped with professionally trained staff able to assist both the court
and the parties appearing before it in all matters requiring social work services and
advice, and in particular the court would provide good facilities for 'conciliation'
meetings between the parties.[4]

Finer's concept of conciliation

The Finer report effectively (and it must be said by means of assertion rather than
reasoned argument) rejected the traditional view that 'conciliation' meant what it
had meant for the 1936 Harris Committee for Lord Merriman and for the Denning
Committee: that is, that it was primarily aimed at bringing about a 'reconciliation'
between husband and wife. For Finer, conciliation was concerned rather with
'engendering common sense, reasonableness and agreement in dealing with the
consequences of estrangement',[5] and its objective was to empower families 'to
make the best decisions and reach the best solutions over the whole range of
problems' which breakdown involved, placing primary emphasis on the 'practical
needs of the family at the time when the court assumes control over the
relationship between its members and their affairs'. This was based on an ideology
which would probably have seemed shocking to most members of the 1956 *Royal
Commission on Marriage and Divorce* (to go back no further in time): Finer urged

---

[1]   1917–1974

[2]   1921–1997. McGregor, a distinguished scholar, had a particular interest in the influence of the law
     on society. An erudite and passionate advocate of divorce and other law reform, he was Professor
     of Social Institutions in London University, director of the Bedford College Socio-Legal Research
     Unit and a member of a number of influential government committees in the 1960s and 1970s.

[3]   *Report of the Committee on One-Parent Families*, Cmnd 5629 (July 1974).

[4]   Ibid, para 4.283(3) and (4).

[5]   Ibid.

that divorce was simply a recognition of a *fact*; and the victims of family breakdown should be *encouraged* to 'wind up their failure with the least possible recrimination, and to make the most rational and efficient arrangements possible for their own and their children's future'.

The origins of Bristol Family Mediation

The old fashioned moralist (if any survived the 'swinging sixties') might have said that this sounded more like a process intended to facilitate well-structured company re-organisations than a process intended to deal with marriage and thus with the fundamental basis of all civilised social systems.[1] However, in 1974 Finer's ideas had a powerful resonance with many – including judges, practising lawyers and social workers – confronting the reality of marital breakdown and concerned to civilise the legal arrangements for what was certainly no longer (if it ever had been) a rarity; and the Bristol group which formed a Finer Joint Action Committee in 1974 was different from similar groups elsewhere only in the pertinacity and effectiveness of its activities. Accounts of the circumstances in which what was originally called the Bristol Courts Family Conciliation Service was established in 1979 will be found in later chapters of this book,[2] and it is perhaps appropriate for someone who had no involvement at the time to emphasise how historic an event the birth of the Service was and how substantial the achievement of those who surmounted difficulties which would certainly have deterred less able and skilful men and women. The very fact that a full-time service had been established, so that a Conciliation Service could be seen to be a practical and functioning reality, encouraged others to act; and it also prompted analysis, discussion and debate about what could and what could not (or should not) be done.

But it is important to remember that the concept of Finer-style 'conciliation' also had an appeal to Governments concerned to reduce the ever-increasing cost of financing litigation over the financial and custody matters which the legislation had left to the courts. The Divorce Reform Act, as administered under the Special Procedure, had made husband and wife the only real judges of whether the marriage should be ended; and it increasingly seemed that 'conciliation' could also help in allowing the courts to shed much of the burden of involvement in regulating the consequences. This approach was exemplified in a 1979 *Practice Direction*[3] which noted that 'under a Registrar's guidance' a pre-trial review could often lead the parties in defended cases 'to compose their differences' or at least 'drop insubstantial charges and defences, and to concentrate on the main issues in dispute'. The desirability of assisting husband and wife to 'settle their differences without recourse to formal court procedures' became a recurrent and insistent theme of Government pronouncements; and what appealed to civil servants and some lawyers about 'conciliation' as re-defined by Finer was that it seemed to deal

---

[1]   *Dodd v Dodd* [1906] P 189, at 205, per Gorell Barnes P (not, as it happens, an 'old fashioned moralist', but the chairman of the *Royal Commission on Marriage and Divorce* Cmnd 6478 whose report provided the blue-print for what was at the time regarded as radical reform of the divorce laws, not effected until the Matrimonial Causes Act 1937).

[2]   See especially Chapters 2 and 3.

[3]   *Practice Direction (Divorce: Directions for Trials)* [1979] 1 WLR 2.

in real and indeed measurable outcomes, rather than with the less easily definable benefits often claimed for counselling and other social work activities. No doubt it was for that reason that – as revealed by Lisa Parkinson[1] – officials advised the Bristol Team to use the Finer definition in their initial application for funding.

Conciliation schemes and the courts

The Bristol Scheme was independent of the courts and other State agencies;[2] but it had a *relationship* with the courts and court users, as indeed was evidenced by the reference to 'Court' in the original title. But quite what was that relationship to be? It soon emerged that there was a danger that 'conciliation' as a term connoting an activity deserving of direct public support would become restricted to work specifically related to court proceedings; and indeed, when the Thatcher government finally responded to pressure for an official investigation of what could be achieved by conciliation, that term was closely defined as being the 'provision of facilities and services to assist the parties to actual or potential matrimonial proceedings' to achieve a settlement of their disputes.[3] In 1983, the Committee which the government had appointed duly reported that conciliation was best provided as an adjunct to the court system, possibly combined with procedural changes designed to encourage early settlement; and that accordingly, since 'out-of-court' schemes did not 'save money overall' and were 'less cost-effective than in-court schemes', no central government funding for services such as BCFCS could be justified.

Critics soon pointed out the inadequacies of the Committee's analysis and, in the event, probably its only long-term effect was to ensure that a formal distinction between 'in-court' and 'out-of-court' conciliation became firmly established.[4] Both kinds of 'conciliation' flourished. 'Out-of-court' conciliation (renamed 'mediation') enjoyed powerful support,[5] whilst 'in-court' conciliation (also increasingly called 'mediation') was increasingly directed to procedural changes intended to facilitate settlement,[6] and indeed 'mediation' is now officially recognised as a desirable form of dispute resolution over a wide range of civil litigation.[7] Many flowers have bloomed; yet there remain not only the practical

---

[1]   See p 34.

[2]   In 1947 the Denning Committee (*Final Report of the Committee on Procedure in Matrimonial Causes* Cmnd 7024, at 1947, para 25) had emphasised that, to 'appeal to the Englishman's character' it was necessary for reconciliation facilities to be 'removed as far as possible from any suspicion of official supervision or interference in the private affairs of individuals'. The Committee evidently accepted the view that 'better class parties would not readily turn to probation officers or a state service' and that for this reason 'voluntary workers of superior class' were to be preferred in this role: see note on PRO file HO45/25202.

[3]   *Report of the Inter-Departmental Committee on Conciliation* (1983). The Committee was established in direct response to a recommendation by the Law Commission: *The Financial Consequences of Divorce* (1981) Law Com No 112, para 13.

[4]   See M Murch, p 30 below.

[5]   Notably from the Children Act Advisory Committee, the Law Commission and the Lord Chancellor's Legal Aid Advisory Committee. Statutory recognition was given by Family Law Act 1996.

[6]   Notably the Financial Dispute Resolution procedure introduced by the Family Proceedings (Amendment) (No 2) Rules 1999.

[7]   See R Bird at Chapter 5 below

difficulties of providing services without assurances of long-term funding, but also an uneasy ambiguity about the extent to which the law is prepared to allow 'private-ordering' to be conclusive in the context of family breakdown. And that is only part of an even more profound question: what is the legitimate role of the courts, which by definition embody the coercive judicial power of the state,[1] in what was traditionally regarded as the private realm of family life?

---

[1] Contempt of Court Act 1981, s 19. In the 14th Annual Law Faculty Lecture delivered at the University of Bristol on 21 November 2002, and published under the title 'The Law and the Family' in [2003] *Common Law World Review*, at 101–116, I suggested that in general family relationships are more likely to be damaged by the intervention of this coercive power than mended.

Chapter 2

THE GERM AND THE GEM OF AN IDEA

Professor Mervyn Murch

Introduction

In the previous chapter, Stephen Cretney in his inimitable way considered the historical and political context which gave rise to the development of mediation in the United Kingdom during the second half of the twentieth century. In this chapter I narrow the focus to recount and reflect upon the beginnings of the Bristol Courts Family Conciliation Service (BCFCS) which became a national exemplar. Because I was one of the people involved more than a quarter of a century ago, I have had to rack my memory and tread the tightrope between subjective involvement and historical accuracy. Fortunately I have been able to refer to various working papers compiled at the time and to some official publications and have consulted with some former colleagues who were also involved.

I start with a brief recapitulation and comment on the Finer Committee's view of conciliation.[1] I explain how this stimulated a small group of Bristol family justice practitioners and myself to convene a conference at Bristol University. This examined what Finer had to say about the need for a unified system of family courts and the place of conciliation within it. It also considered some initial findings from research which I had recently conducted concerning the circumstances of families in divorce proceedings. From this conference emerged a sub-group which took steps to set up the BCFCS on an experimental basis. The chapter concludes with a reflective assessment.

Sowing the seeds

(a) Social change and social reform in the 1970s

The first chapter of this book explained how by the end of the 1970s, the incidence of divorce was again rising rapidly.[2] With the provision of civil legal aid for divorce[3] social reformers and government officials were searching for economies while civilising the divorce process. Rapidly changing social values were prompting vigorous debates about the nature of divorce law, the social, economic and legal disadvantages of women and single parents, and the effects of marriage breakdown on children. There was growing recognition that English family law

---

[1] Department of Health and Social Security, July 1974 *Report of the Committee on One-Parent Families (Chairman, the Honourable Sir Morris Finer)* Cmnd 5629 HMSO.

[2] The number of divorce petitions filed in 1970 was 70,575 and rose by 1977 to 167,034, two-thirds of which involved families with dependent children.

[3] The cost to the tax payer leapt sharply from £11.5m in 1971/72 to £34.5m in 1976/77 – the greater part of which was spent on matrimonial causes.

had become a jungle of ad hoc rules, procedures and remedies exercisable in a wide variety of courts with different and sometimes overlapping jurisdictions. Both the new Law Commission under its first Chairman, Sir Leslie Scarman (as he then was), and the Committee on One Parent Families, under the Chairmanship of Sir Morris Finer, both High Court judges with experience of family proceedings, were attracted to the idea of a unified system of local family courts.[1] At the time, opinion differed over such matters as the composition of the court (should magistrates have a role); which government department should be responsible; and how associated court welfare support services might be organised.

(b)   Finer Committee's concept of conciliation

The Finer Committee's interest in conciliation stemmed from a belief that the fragmented structure of the courts – and particularly the stigmatic criminal overtones of the magistrates' domestic jurisdiction – coupled with the traditional adversarial model of civil litigation was not only expensive but inimical to settling family conflicts. Drawing on material from overseas – particularly Australia, New Zealand and the United States, as well as emerging findings from my own study of families in divorce proceedings – it concluded that once proceedings had begun, procedures to promote *reconciliation* were largely ineffective whereas *conciliation* had 'a substantial success in civilising the consequences of marriage breakdown'.[2] The Committee was at pains to distinguish conciliation from reconciliation, stating:

> 'By "reconciliation" we mean the reuniting of the spouses. By "conciliation" we mean assisting the parties to deal with the consequences of their marriage breakdown, whether resulting from divorce or separation, by reaching agreements or giving consents or reducing the area of conflict upon custody, support, access to and education of children, financial provision, the disposition of the matrimonial home, lawyers' fees and every other matter arising from the breakdown which calls for a decision on future arrangements.'[3]

(c)   The influence of family law research at Bristol University

From 1972 to 1975 while the Finer Committee was receiving evidence, an empirical socio-legal research into the circumstances of families affected by divorce, funded by the Social Science Research Council (as it then was) took place at Bristol University under my direction. The idea for this study arose from a conversation between myself and Sir Leslie Scarman at a conference at Dartington Hall in 1971, organised by the Joint Law Commission Home Office Working Party on Family Courts. Scarman was keen to harness social research to the Commission's programme of family law reform, a view which in those days did not find favour in the Lord Chancellor's Department. With the exception of a noticeable study of the domestic jurisdiction of magistrates' courts by McGregor,

---

[1]   A joint Home Office/Law Commission Working Party on Family Courts was established about 1971. Its work was never finished because the Home Office and Lord Chancellor's Department took different views about the future of the domestic jurisdiction of magistrates' courts. Subsequently it was said that the Finer Committee 'stole the clothes' of this working party when it undertook its own examination of the family court issue.

[2]   Op cit, para 4:311, p 185.

[3]   Home Office/Law Commission Working Party on Family Courts para 4:288, p 176.

Blom-Cooper and Gibson,[1] the available literature at the time showed that there was an almost complete dearth of reliable consumer views of the legal and social services associated with divorce.

The Bristol study, conducted in the South West of England with the help of local divorce court welfare services, used a combination of observation of the then open hearings of undefended divorce petitions and follow-up interviews with representative samples of parents.[2] Although intended as an investigation of the impact of divorce on families, it also focused on the operation of the so-called welfare check in uncontested divorce proceedings and the work of the court welfare service[3] as experienced by 42 divorcing couples whose children have been the subject of welfare reports.

The material which came from this court welfare sample emphasised the potential importance of 'conciliation'. These were cases which mainly involved serious custody disputes. Although the overt justification for the welfare officers' intervention was the need for a welfare report, it seemed from the accounts of many of the parents that the welfare officer also performed other informal, less explicitly authorised tasks. These were classified as:

– cathartic listening – an offloading of pent-up stress to an empathetic neutral person;
– mediation – settling or working on the more emotionally inflamed aspects of parental conflict with the help of an impartial mediator;
– child advocacy – interpreting the children's views both to the judge and to the parents;
– 'passage agent' family-minded support ie – acting as an informal guide through the critical transitions following parental separation and the associated uncertainties of proceedings; .
– a certain amount of welfare rights advice.

All these tasks seem directed at helping the family as a whole deal with the consequences of marriage breakdown and were therefore consistent with the Finer Committee's broad concept of conciliation.

The research also revealed those characteristics of the court welfare officers' manner and approach which the parents most appreciated. These have been explained more fully elsewhere.[4] I summarise them here since they influenced our thinking about what should be looked for in potential conciliators.

The desired characteristics were first and foremost an impartial non-judgemental manner. Court welfare officers, like judges, were clearly expected to remain

---

[1]   OR McGregor, L Blom-Cooper and C Gibson C *Separated Spouses* (Duckworth, 1970).
[2]   L Elston, J Fuller and M Murch 'Judicial Hearings of Undefended Divorce Petitions' (1975) *Modern Law Review* vol 38, p 632.
[3]   M Murch *Justice and Welfare in Divorce* (Sweet & Maxwell, 1980).
[4]   See M Murch *Justice and Welfare in Divorce* (Sweet & Maxwell, 1980), at pp 172–182.

impartial in any conflict between parents. In this they differed from the protective partisan stance which clients expected of their solicitors.[1] As I commented later:

> 'Curiously, even parents involved even in the most acrimonious conflict, seemed to retain a sense of an elusive middle ground between them which with skill and understanding, could be identified by someone who was fair and impartial.'

It seems as if many people involved in conflict (perhaps only in their more reflective, calmer moments) sense that their perceptions of each other have become in some way distorted and often welcome the agency of concerned outsiders in their attempts to correct that distortion.

Secondly, parents particularly appreciated the court welfare officers' concern for the family as a whole. In this respect, it may have been significant that most of the welfare officers were themselves married parents. This seemed to lead to a more immediate identification with the parents which in turn appeared to increase the parents' confidence in the officers.

Thirdly, it was noticeable that the parents did not view the divorce court welfare officers stigmatically – unlike their view of local authority social services departments, the probation service and to an extent the marriage guidance council.[2]

Fourthly, parents responded positively to welfare officers who had an open no nonsense manner. Straightforwardness coupled with sensibility increased parents trust in the officer and made it easier for them to share their personal concerns and anxieties. In several cases this seems to have made more acceptable those parts of the welfare officers' findings which conflicted with the parents' individual aspirations and interests. By contrast, a detached sceptical manner aroused mistrust, anxiety and sometimes outright hostility.

Overall, therefore, where officers fulfilled these expectations, they were seen as complementing the partisan support and protective negotiating skill of the parents' solicitors. We concluded that they were playing a valuable role in helping estranged parents focus on the future care of their children, clearing some of the emotional undergrowth which was entangling the family, obstructing communications both between the parents and with their children, and preventing the family as a whole from reorganising itself on the basis of a fair division of matrimonial assets and appropriate arrangements for the children.

The one major complaint of these 'satisfied parents' was that the court welfare officer had come on the scene much too late. This was because child-related disputes where the court asked for a welfare report were generally heard months after the hearing of the divorce petition. We concluded that 'conciliation' of this kind would have been more valuable in the early stages of marriage breakdown,

---

[1]   For an in-depth analysis of this distinction see G Davis *Partisans and Mediators* (Clarendon Press, 1988).

[2]   M Murch *Justice and Welfare in Divorce* (Sweet & Maxwell, 1980), at pp 175–179.

ideally soon after the crisis of parental separation or when one of the parents had consulted a solicitor.

An experiment on a shoestring – establishing the Bristol Courts Family Conciliation Service

(i)   The Finer Joint Action Committee 1974

In the autumn of 1974, spurred on by the publication of the Finer Committee Report and the emerging results of the Bristol research summarised above, a small group comprising two solicitors (David Burrows and Paul Mildred), an assistant chief probation officer (Tony Wells), and myself organised a conference of local practitioners, chaired by the senior local county court judge, His Honour Judge Russell. It was held in the Senior Common Room of Bristol University. As I recall, about 60 people attended, mostly local solicitors, several county court registrars (now known as district judges), representatives from the probation service, some local authority social workers, marriage guidance counsellors and several academics. A working group calling itself the Bristol Finer Joint Action Committee was set up charged with the task of drawing up plans for an experimental scheme linked to the courts based on Finer's concept of conciliation. The scheme would incorporate features suggested by the Bristol research concerning 'conciliation' as practised informally by court welfare officers. The aim was to see whether a non-stigmatic confidential service could be established which would attract couples in the early pre-litigation stage of divorce so that they and their legal advisers could be helped to reach settlement about child-related matters. This would obviously involve winning the confidence of local solicitors and the courts so that they would refer clients.

The challenge of setting up such a service was formidable. Initially there was no money to fund the venture and it was recognised that to start with, even if suitably qualified and experienced people could be persuaded to staff the service, they might have to do so on a voluntary basis. Suitable accommodation with an interview room and a secure office would have to be found. Above all, solicitors, a cautious and traditional profession, would have to be persuaded that the venture was likely to be sufficiently reliable and competent in order to take the chance of referring clients to it. On a practical level it was recognised that a co-ordinator would be needed to link conciliators with solicitors and their clients and to undertake a certain amount of publicity. A part-time secretary might also be needed.

The first step was to establish a management committee. Because initially the aim was to follow Finer's concept of conciliation with an expectation that in time local family courts would be set up, it was agreed that the local judiciary would be represented on the Committee. Accordingly, it was chaired by Judge Russell. Other members included two county court registrars, the clerk to the justices, two magistrates from the local domestic bench, the chief probation officer for Avon and the senior divorce court welfare officer, a barrister and representatives of the Bristol Law Society, several voluntary social work agencies and the marriage guidance council. The active endorsement of the local judiciary, particularly Judge

Russell, and the senior county court registrar, Geoffrey Parmiter, was crucial in winning the confidence of solicitors.

From the start, the service was conceived as pioneering a new form of collaboration between lawyers and specialist conciliators. This would not only benefit separating and divorcing couples and their children, but it was thought that it would also facilitate the solicitors' task of negotiating a settlement and reduce the burden of litigation in the courts. As was stated in a subsequent committee working document:

> 'Many people are too distressed and confused when their marriage breaks down to give their solicitors clear instructions. There is a need for clarification before legal proceedings are commenced, since the position taken up by one parent depends on his/her perception of the other party's position. A conciliator, who is in touch with *both* parties at an early stage, can establish what is agreed and what is contested, and help them to come to terms with emotions which may be hindering or blocking a settlement. This is the first stage of the conciliation process, the second being the negotiation over issues which are identified as contested.'

(ii)   Recruiting the first conciliators

From the beginning the management committee agreed that conciliators would have to be qualified and experienced social workers or marriage guidance counsellors. It was understood that they would need to be given additional specialist training, consultation and support. The giving of legal advice would not be part of the conciliator's function.

Bristol was fortunate in that two local voluntary organisations offered the services of a small group of suitably qualified people willing to commit themselves to this experimental venture, initially on an unpaid basis; the local marriage guidance council and a group of unemployed but trained social workers from an organisation known as the Third Hand. This had been started by a recently retired social work tutor from Exeter University, Joan Eastman. She had the idea that there might be a number of trained women social workers living locally who had 'retired' in order to start families and who might be looking for part-time work as a way of keeping 'their hand in'. She was successful in recruiting what she termed a 'rust-proofing' group of this kind and indeed, before conciliation came on the scene, it had provided several part-time medical social workers attached to a progressive medical group practice in the City – a scheme which was monitored for the Department of Health. Four members of the Third Hand volunteered to help start the BCFCS including Kay Begg who was to become a leading figure when conciliation became a national movement and Lisa Parkinson who with others was involved in the setting up of National Family Conciliation Council (later known as National Family Mediation).[1] In addition, two marriage guidance counsellors volunteered and were appointed.

The first unpaid volunteer co-ordinator of the service was Daphne Norbury, previously a tutor to Bristol University's postgraduate generic applied social

---

[1]   Lisa would carry the flame of UK conciliation into the international field.

studies course for social workers. She specialised in child care and family studies, and had recent experience of divorce court welfare work at the Royal Courts of Justice. She had also undertaken an advanced social casework course at the Tavistock Clinic.[1] Daphne held the fort until the Committee could secure funds to support Lisa Parkinson as the service's co-ordinator, a responsibility she shared for a few months with Kay Begg.

(iii)   Staff selection, training, consultation and support

Once the management committee had agreed a development plan to launch the service, the first step was to invite applications for appointment as conciliators from the Third Hand and the Local Marriage Guidance Council and the marriage guidance council. After a shortlist had been compiled, selected applicants were interviewed by a sub-group of the management committee. They were also seen by Daphne Norbury, co-ordinator, but a final decision was not made until Mrs Judith Stephens, a consultant to the service, had seen all the candidates. The Committee and the conciliators themselves thought it important that they should receive regular supervision and the support of a specialist consultant who agreed to visit the service on a monthly basis. Judith Stephens, formerly a principal psychiatric social worker at the Tavistock Clinic, London, was also a regional consultant to the National Marriage Guidance Council and had experience of providing seminars on marital and family interaction for probation officers and divorce court welfare officers in the South West region.[2]

Although all conciliators were qualified social workers or marriage guidance counsellors, it was recognised that they would need to be well prepared to work in the new context of family proceedings. Thus one of the first tasks was to provide them with reading materials and family law seminars backed up by group discussions in preparation for engaging with their first cases. During this initial training period, they received no payment, although the management committee and the co-ordinator were seeking funding for the service. Once the initial grant was received from a local charity, they were paid at a reduced rate for the first year.[3]

(iv)   Fundraising and finding office accommodation

Raising funds for conciliation services was to prove a major problem throughout the first decade or so of the life of BCFCS. To some extent, being the first in the field and therefore a groundbreaking initiative, it was easier to attract funds from charitable sources. Later, once similar services developed around the country, it became harder to convince charities of the need for continued support. Thus pressure for government funding increased.

---

[1]   She was subsequently to become deputy director of the British Association for Adoption and Fostering (BAAF).

[2]   She was also a visiting lecturer to the postgraduate generic applied social studies course at Bristol University.

[3]   Inter-departmental Committee on Conciliation (1982) *Study Group Report* p 59, Lord Chancellor's Department.

As far as the Bristol service was concerned, the management committee decided that initially it might be easier to approach a local charity for modest launch aid funding. If it proved successful then a further approach to a national foundation for a larger grant might be the way forward. The first grant of £1,250 was from the Sir Halley Stewart Trust to cover the first year's operation and the lease of an interviewing room. Subsequently, grants were received from the Van Neste Trust and the Nuffield Foundation.

(v)   *Launching the service*

It took some time during 1976 and 1977 for the management committee to formulate a viable plan of operation. Much of the time was taken up with deciding how to fund the service, how to promote it locally, and with recruiting and training the first group of conciliators. By the end of 1977 arrangements were in place to launch the scheme as a part-time service. It began in February 1978 and by May 1979 sufficient funds from the Nuffield Foundation had been secured to run the service for a 3-year period as a fully operational service, enabling Lisa Parkinson to be confirmed as the co-ordinator. Office accommodation close to the courts and to many solicitors offices was eventually found with the help of the local probation service. It comprised a general office, a small office for the co-ordinator and an interview room which was furnished informally with books and toys provided for children. As far as I remember, rent was waived for the first few months and thereafter for a period was nominal.

Some reflections

Looking back from my perspective as a socio-legal family law researcher, a number of questions are prompted:

– Would we have attempted it if we had known all the difficulties that lay ahead?
– How far was the original Finer concept followed?
– Should conciliation be seen as integral to the infrastructure of the family justice system and as part of the welfare support services for the courts?
– Rather, is it primarily part of the 'private ordering' of family disputes and therefore essentially an alternative to the public provision of family justice via the courts?
– Should children have a voice in the conciliation process?

Perhaps the first question to be considered is what was it in the spirit of the times which attracted so many local Bristol practitioners to the original idea and maintained their support for it when times became difficult? To answer that question one has to remember that 1974/75 was probably the high water mark of the great post-war period of social change and social reform. The scale of marriage breakdown had risen to such an extent that few extended families did not have at least some experience of a relative who had been, or was in the process of, divorce. Thus, this was a period when private troubles on a massive scale became a public concern – perhaps more so than today when divorce, parental relationship breakdown and family reconstruction have become almost an accepted aspect of family life, however stressful it can be.

A further factor was that in professional circles – social work, medicine and increasingly specialist family law, there was a growing interest and understanding of the psychodynamics of family life. This fostered a belief that a counselling or quasi-psychotherapeutic approach could ease some of the more destructive tensions associated with this major life-changing event. The hope was that this would enable people to work out fair and reasonable arrangements for their families' future. Moreover, at that time there was still a strong belief amongst practitioners that the State's resources should be devoted to supportive intervention of this kind. Many also believed that conciliation held out the prospect of avoiding unnecessary legal expense and the risks associated with litigation – one reason why in the early days the Lord Chancellor's Legal Aid Advisory Committee took such an interest in the experimental Bristol scheme.[1]

Some would now say that all this was rather naïve and characteristic of a middle-class modernist approach to life which has been largely superseded by our post-modern commercial consumerist society with its individualism and fragmentation of social structures.[2] Whatever the case, the tide of social reform was certainly to change within a few months when the country was hit by the major economic recession caused by the oil crisis of 1975 which followed the Yom Kippur war. Before long the Thatcher government was to pursue social policies of retrenchment, the rhetoric for which at least was dedicated to rolling back the frontiers of the State and leaving social welfare initiatives largely to the voluntary sector. This also of course increased competition for limited charitable funds. Such a policy was only moderated as far as family law was concerned when, following the Child Care Law Review, Lord Mackay, the new Lord Chancellor and Virginia Bottomley, Secretary of State for Health, were responsible for legislating the Children Act 1989 and committing the government to a rolling programme of family law reform.

Another important question is why the BCFCS initiative so quickly narrowed the focus of its work from the broad Finer concept of conciliation within a family court context to a more limited out-of-court mediation scheme? Likewise, why was a separate in-court scheme subsequently developed by the local probation service in association with county court officials?[3] John Westcott pointed out in a paper written in December 1983 that this first became a *contentious* issue after the widely

---

[1] Lord Chancellor's Office (1979) *28th Legal Aid Annual Report (1977–78)*, p 91, HMSO. See also Lord Chancellor's Office (1980) *29th Legal Aid Annual Report (1978–79)*, p 82, HMSO. Also Lord Chancellor's Office (1981) *30th Legal Aid Annual Report (1979–80)*, pp 99–101 and 120–124, HMSO.

[2] See further, Z Bauman *Life in Fragments: Essays in Post-modern Ethics* chapter 3 'Broken Lives Broken Strategies' (Blackwell/Oxford, 1995). Also U Beck U and E Beck-Gernsheim *The Normal Chaos of Love* (Polity Press, 1995).

[3] For more detailed discussion of this issue see M Murch and D Hooper *The Family Justice System*, chapter 8 'Does conciliation have a place in the family justice system?' (Family Law, 1992), at pp 83–92.

criticised inter-departmental report (the Robinson Report) was published in 1983. Westcott observed:

> 'It might well be that an unfortunate and artificial demarcation between in-court and out-of-court conciliation has arisen in Bristol (and we need not necessarily speculate on the reasons for this).'[1]

Whatever the case, the combined effect of these two developments seems to have established a divided model that exists to this day.

Another consequence was that it seems to have set out-of-court mediators apart professionally from those social workers (former divorce court welfare officers and guardians ad litem) who now work within the unified Child and Family Court Advisory and Support Service (CAFCASS). In this context it is interesting to note that despite the initial organisational problems which beset CAFCASS, it is now experimenting with three mediation schemes as part of its support service function.

Looking back, it is clear that Westcott was not alone in being worried by the split between the in-court and out-of-court schemes in Bristol. Some of us agreed with him that if a family court was to become a reality, 'the ideal framework' would be for all conciliators to be attached to it, with, as he put it:

> 'Some conciliating couples being referred to them by the court (in-court) and some making themselves available on the direct request of couples who had not necessarily started proceedings (out-of-court). On the face of it there would be no need for any governing body or committee as conciliation would be done within the framework of the court.'[2]

As it was, Finer's concept of a local family court was to prove something of a mirage given the adverse economic climate that soon developed, even though to this day the idea has not completely vanished and there are even current rumours that Government is reconsidering the matter.

Another reason of course for Bristol's initial focus on mediation was the need to set realistic priorities given the extreme shortage of funds. It has also been suggested to me recently that the first co-ordinator and conciliators encountered a certain male chauvinist scepticism when the scheme was first suggested to the local probation service. Evidently, some probation officers took a dim view of a service being staffed by a small team of part-time women volunteers and which might be seen as offering a rival service to probation's civil domestic work. However that may be, one has to remember that the first Bristol conciliators were breaking into what was for them an unexplored domain then dominated by the well-established and socially high status legal profession, and this was a field where divorce court welfare work was still struggling to stake a claim.[3] As such the new conciliators

---

[1]   Private correspondence with John Westcott.

[2]   Ibid.

[3]   It is worth noting that conciliation was practised by probation officers with cases referred from the magistrates' courts even before the Second World War. See Home Office *Memorandum on the*

had to quickly fashion out and negotiate an acceptable role for themselves, adapting their social work or marriage guidance training to an entirely new setting. Not only did they have to win the trust and confidence of solicitors and court officials if conciliating couples were to be referred to them, the clients too had to be won over since they authorised the work. Thus, conciliators could not be directly compared with court welfare officers who derived their statutory authority primarily from the court and whose formal task was to report on the children's circumstances. In retrospect we might have underestimated this important distinction. Our minds were firmly fixed on the relatively simple idea of finding ways of providing a Finer-type conciliation service in the initial stages of divorce proceedings.

Another factor that may have encouraged the first Bristol conciliators to concentrate on mediation between the parents was the fact that their first professional consultant, Mrs Judith Stephens, had worked with the Tavistock Clinic's Family Discussion Bureau (later to become the Tavistock Institute of Marital Studies) with its psychoanalytic slant on the psychodynamics of marital interaction.[1] Consciously or unconsciously this probably influenced, in particular, the conciliators with a marriage guidance background through their identification with the consultant. It certainly seems to have caused them to focus on the marital relationship rather than attempting to work directly with the whole family including the children, although in the early days Kay Begg and Lisa Parkinson involved some children in the conciliation process if their parents agreed.[2] Moreover, as most of the referrals were to come from solicitors who represented individual parents and who were attempting to negotiate between them, it was understandable that conciliators would, as it were, follow suit.

As far as children are concerned, they were the focus of the court welfare officers intervention and, when old enough to understand, were usually consulted during the course of the inquiries for the court. Nevertheless, it is only now beginning to be fully recognised that, in divorce proceedings as a whole, children often feel ill-informed and excluded when their parents' relationship breaks down. Certainly, as I saw it, the first BCFCS conciliators and the management committee did not fully appreciate this point and so rather ignored that aspect of the research findings at the time which showed how court welfare officers often reopened channels of communication between the parents and the children.

Principles and Practice in the Work of Matrimonial Conciliation in Magistrates' Courts (HMSO, 1948). See also M Murch (1980) op cit.

[1] See H Dicks, *Marital Tensions* (RKP, 1967). Also L Pincus et al *Marriage: Studies in Emotional Conflict and Growth* (Methuen 1968). Also K Bannister and L Pincus *Shared Phantasy in Marital Problems – therapy in four person relationships* (Tavistock Institute for Human Relations/Codicote Press, 1965).

[2] It should also be remembered that at this time in the UK psychodynamic systems thinking and family therapy upon which it was based was in its infancy although developing rapidly in the United States. But see L Parkinson 'Conciliation: A New Approach to Family Conflict Resolution' (1983) *British Journal of Social Work,* vol 13, pp 20–37, for examples where conciliation involved children using a family system's perspective.

Again, the exclusion of children from direct participation in the mediation process, although not deliberately intended in the early days of BCFCS, might well have influenced what was to become a feature of most mediation services operating in the 1990s. Thus, a national survey conducted for the Lord Chancellor's Department[1] revealed that children are seldom directly consulted. Nevertheless, in recent years there has been a growing body of research[2] indicating not only that children often feel excluded from the divorce process but that this increases their stress and anxieties. Also, several studies[3] have shown that many divorcing parents find it difficult to talk to the children about their separation. The problems of principle and practice involved in developing family justice procedures which can give effect to the general principle that the voice of the child should be heard have been considered elsewhere.[4]

A final point. Those of us who helped to set up BCFCS would have been amazed how sophisticated mediation became and how rapidly it was professionalised,[5] spawning a variety of specialist and sometimes conflicting schools of thought as to what constitutes good practice, ie single mediators or co-mediators, single issue or all issue mediation, in-court and out-of-court schemes and such like. Present day arrangements for training, qualification, accreditation as well as recognition and regulation by organisations such as National Family Mediation, the UK College of Mediators and the Legal Services Commission are all a far cry from our initial concept of simply finding some volunteer social workers and counsellors to work with families on conflict resolution in collaboration with their solicitors in the early stages of proceedings.

---

[1]   M Murch and G Douglas et al, *Safeguarding Children's Welfare in Uncontentious Divorce: a study of s 41 of the Matrimonial Act 1973* (Lord Chancellor's Department Research Series 7/99, 1999). This study, which involved a survey of all then existing mediation schemes, reported that 'mediators are, as one would expect, highly aware of the importance of making parents aware of their children's views and feelings. However, they prefer to do this within the mediation process by suggesting to parents that they put themselves in the children's position and empathise with them… As a professional group, mediators appear to have weighed the advantages and disadvantages of direct consultation with children and concluded that it is undesirable as a matter of routine since mediation is defined as a process concerned with assisting *adult* disputants improve their communication with each other and to reach agreement'.

[2]   See, for example, (i) C Lyons, E Surrey, J Timms, *Effective Support Services for Children and Young Persons When Parental Relationships Break Down* (Caloust Gulbenkian Foundation/Liverpool University, 1999); (ii) J Buchanan, J Hunt, H Bretherton, V Bream, *Families in Conflict: Perspectives of Children and Parents of the Court Welfare Service* (Policy Press, 2001); (iii) I Butler, L Scanlan, M Robinson, G Douglas, M Murch M, *Divorcing Children – Children's Experience of Their Parents Divorce* (Jessica Kingsley Publishers, 2003). For international comparisons see J Pryor, B Rogers *Children in Changing Families, Life After Parental Separation* (Blackwell, 2001).

[3]   See I Butler et al op cit, pp 33–58.

[4]   N Lowe and M Murch, *Children's Participation in the Family Justice System: Translating Principles into Practice* (2001) CFLQ vol 13 no 2 at p 137. Updated and reproduced in J Dewar and S Parker, *Family Law: Processes, Practices, Pressures* (Hart Publishing, 2003).

[5]   In this respect the way mediation became 'professional' matches a similar process that occurred with guardians ad litem once the State funded separate representation for parents and children in public law care proceedings in the 1980s.

Chapter 3

FAMILY MEDIATION IN PRACTICE 'A HAPPY CONCATENATION'?

Lisa Parkinson

The pilot scheme – 1977 onwards

As Stephen Cretney and Mervyn Murch have explained in their interesting chapters on developments in family law and the origins of family conciliation in Bristol, the proposal for a family conciliation service attracted strong support, but putting it into practice posed difficult questions. Who would do the conciliating? Where would the service be based? How could it be funded? How would it complement the work of the divorce court welfare service and marriage guidance councils? What relationship, if any, would there be with the courts?

During 1977 four qualified social workers and three experienced marriage guidance counsellors were recruited and appointed as part-time conciliators, making a team of seven part-time conciliators.[1] We were willing to work unpaid for a few months while the search for funding continued. We embarked on some preliminary training, including role-plays (later a key element in formal mediation training). We drew from our training and experience in working with separated parents, couples and families but from the outset we recognised that the role of family conciliator or mediator needs to be clearly defined and distinguished from the different roles of social worker, counsellor or court reporter. We met regularly in each other's homes and in January 1978, with the support of our consultant, Daphne Norbury, we drew up the aims of the family conciliation service and defined its basic principles. A cardinal principle was that conciliators, unlike divorce court welfare officers and local authority social workers, have no statutory powers and no inquisitorial functions. The service would be confidential (except where a child was believed to be at risk of serious harm). In maintaining an impartial and non-directive position, the conciliator's aim was to facilitate informal, face-to-face discussions between separating and divorcing parents to help them reach their own, agreed decisions. In this way, parents could avoid contested applications over their children in situations that would otherwise be increasingly managed by their solicitors and potentially determined by the court.

There was jubilation in February 1978 when the embryo service obtained its first grant – £1,250 from the Van Neste Trust. The Bristol Council for Voluntary Service offered use of a room free of charge for conciliation appointments and

---

[1]   I was one of the four social workers. In 1976 I had been invited to join the steering committee setting up the proposed service. I gave a talk about it in 1977 to fellow members of 'The Third Hand'.

their secretary agreed to take telephone messages and referrals.[1] Leaflets, referral forms and information for clients were distributed, initially to solicitors' firms, explaining the service as :

> 'a pioneer scheme to help separating and divorcing couples to settle disputes, especially over children. It provides a confidential and informal means of clarifying confused situations and reducing conflict, by mediating between the partners before formal proceedings are started.'

During 1978, 26 firms of solicitors referred about 50 cases involving disputes over access and/or child custody.[2] The support from a significant number of solicitors and our initial experience as conciliators encouraged us to continue. There were many meetings, liaison with solicitors and the Probation Service, records and reports. The steering committee met regularly but it was difficult to make further headway without funding. On 1 December 1977 I had caught part of a radio interview with the Solicitor-General, the Hon Peter Archer MP, about the extension of the 'special procedure' in divorce and a possible increase in funding for law centres. 'Or for family conciliation', I wondered. A letter despatched to the Solicitor-General from the committee received an encouraging response and an invitation to a meeting. The meeting took place in London on 9 February 1978 with the Solicitor-General and two officials from the Lord Chancellor's Department. 'A happy concatenation of economy and humanity' was the response to our proposal from a 'Sir Humphrey Appleby' in the Lord Chancellor's Department. We could not help but notice that, in the government's eyes, 'economy' evidently came before 'humanity'.

We were aware of the cost-saving arguments, but the main aims of the service were 'to resolve actual or incipient disputes, especially where children are involved ... and to promote parental co-operation'.[3] We were advised to apply to the Nuffield Foundation for a grant and informed that our application would have the support of the Lord Chancellor's Department. We were instructed by 'Sir Humphrey' to use the term *conciliation*, as defined by the Finer Committee,[4] and we used it synonymously with *mediation*.

Launch of BCFCS as a full-time service, 1 May 1979

At the end of December 1978, the Nuffield Foundation approved a 3-year grant to the Bristol Courts Family Conciliation Service (BCFCS), with full funding in the first year. However, in the second year, the Nuffield grant would be reduced to two-thirds and this would be payable only if the remaining third came from central government. In year 3, the grant would reduce to one-third, payable on condition that the government paid the other two-thirds. The Nuffield Trustees were understandably anxious to secure public funding for conciliation. However, as far

---

[1]   With effect from February 1978 the steering committee asked me to take on the role of acting co-ordinator, to keep records and to report back to the committee, on a voluntary basis.
[2]   Acting co-ordinator's report to BCFCS Management Committee, 1979.
[3]   L Parkinson and J Westcott 'Bristol Courts Family Conciliation Service', *Law Society Gazette*, 21 May 1980.
[4]   *Report of the Committee on One Parent Families* (1974), at para 4.288.

as BCFCS was concerned, the challenge was to make our project known and accepted locally, so that significant take-up of the service and positive results would persuade a reluctant government to provide cash. This had to be done in barely one year. The pressure was enormous. We needed to explain conciliation to the public and solicitors and to other local agencies and to seek well-informed coverage in the media. Above all, we needed to concentrate on developing a highly skilled and specialist service that would facilitate direct communication between separated and often embattled parents, to enable them to reach consensual decisions about current and future arrangements for their children. This is a very hard task for parents who bring intense feelings of anger and loss, insecurity for the future and worries about the consequences for themselves and their children, especially where one parent is seeking separation or divorce against the other's wishes.

The conciliators who had worked unpaid for over a year were paid for conciliation sessions from May 1979 onwards. Two full-time posts were created – a co-ordinator who would also be a conciliator, and a secretary/receptionist.[1] The co-ordinator post was shared initially[2] and one of the conciliators in the pilot project was appointed as secretary/receptionist. Her skills were invaluable in dealing with enquiries and referrals. We rented offices from a firm of estate agents and were about to redecorate them when the roof was taken off the building. Conciliation often felt like that. We bought second-hand office furniture and equipment at bargain prices at an out-of-town warehouse. On 1 May 1979, BCFCS opened its own doors as a full-time service. No sooner had we moved in than a headline in the local paper announced 'Stone fall from danger offices!'. This turned out to be stone falling from the façade of our building. Our landlords did repairs and neither staff nor clients were hit by falling masonry.

The next task was to increase the take-up of conciliation and reassure a still doubtful legal profession that conciliation was complementary to legal advice from solicitors, not a substitute for it. In fact, we referred as many clients to solicitors as they referred to us. Many of our clients needed legal advice but had been reluctant to go to solicitors because they feared incurring legal costs or becoming caught up in legal proceedings. We gave names of solicitors who would take a conciliatory approach if appropriate, rather than an outright adversarial one. This was before the Solicitors Family Law Association was set up. BCFCS hosted meetings for local lawyers to provide further opportunities for them to ask questions and air views. Individual visits to solicitors in central Bristol were invaluable in clearing up misperceptions of conciliation (as counselling or advice giving) and in discussing the kind of circumstances that might be suitable for referral.

Following Daphne Norbury's retirement as our consultant in the autumn of 1978, Judith Stephens from the Tavistock Institute in London became our consultant in May 1979 and we had regular meetings with her, arranged to coincide with her visits to Bristol as Regional Consultant to marriage guidance tutors in the south-west.

---

[1]   These two posts were advertised publicly and interviews were held.
[2]   Initially, Kay Begg worked 2 days per week and I worked 4 days.

The conciliation process – a family-centred approach

By this time, we had a year's experience as conciliators, albeit on a small scale. We were developing a service for families 'in transition' during the upheavals of separation and divorce. We recognised that separation and divorce are not single events: they are processes that take place over time, with the crisis period of separation usually more stressful than the legal divorce, especially for the children concerned. Judith Stephens was very supportive. Mervyn Murch suggests in his chapter that she might have influenced us towards a model of psychodynamic marital counselling, but this was not the case. Family systems theory and some experience in family therapy encouraged the development of a family-centred approach, rather than an adult-focused one. We were aware from the Finer Committee's Report[1] and from research by Eekelaar[2] and others of children's experience of parental divorce and the effects of acrimonious disputes. The needs of children during family break-up were always a priority and, as Kay Begg also explains in her chapter, we sought to help couples maintain their parental role and relationships with their children, while disengaging from their failed marriage or partnership.[3] Most parents did not think it appropriate to involve their children directly in their discussions and it was generally not appropriate to do so at a stage when the parents had not yet decided their own future arrangements. The first priority was to enable parents to reach agreed decisions in which they could co-operate over their children and work out what they needed to explain to their children. Nonetheless, there were cases in which both parents and the conciliator saw benefits for the children in involving them directly. This was not confined to older children. Sometimes younger children were included, but only when the objectives and process of involving them had been carefully discussed and agreed with both parents.[4] In taking this approach and sometimes involving children, the Bristol service may have differed from other conciliation services. Many mediators do not include children at all, although children's and parents' experience of children's involvement is overwhelmingly positive, as long as the objectives and pre-conditions are first worked out carefully with both parents.[5] Whether children are involved directly or indirectly, mediation facilitates better communication between parents and children, as well as between the parents themselves.

A private forum to resolve issues concerning children

Arrangements over children's custody and access (this was well before the Children Act 1989) were of course often inextricably linked with decisions about the future occupation or sale of the family home and other aspects of family finances. These matters were often discussed and agreed in outline, in conjunction with separate legal advice to each party from their solicitors.[6] However, we did not have the necessary knowledge and training at that time to mediate fully on

---

[1]   (Finer) *Report of the Committee on One Parent Families,* Appendix 12 (1974).

[2]   J Eekelaar, *Family Law and Social Policy* (Weidenfeld and Nicolson, 1978).

[3]   L Parkinson, *Conciliation in Separation and Divorce* (Croom Helm, 1986), at p 160.

[4]   For a case example see L Parkinson, 'Conciliation: A New Approach to Family Conflict Resolution' (1982) *British Journal of Social Work* 13 at 30.

[5]   See research studies quoted in L Parkinson *Family Mediation* (Sweet & Maxwell, 1997).

[6]   For case examples, see above.

financial and property issues (this came later, with the direct involvement of solicitors in mediation). To a large extent, the remit of our service coincided with the Finer Committee's concept of conciliation.[1] The main distinction was that the Finer Committee envisaged conciliation under the umbrella of a new family court, whereas BCFCS was community-based and independent of the courts, inviting referrals before court proceedings were commenced, as far as possible. In urgent access and custody cases, conciliation could be undertaken without waiting for legal aid to be granted or a court hearing date to be set. Keenly aware of the risks of being seen as 'do-gooders' or 'the welfare', we asked parents who came to conciliation to define their priorities for their children. Although we believed that, following parental separation, most children need and benefit from continuing relationships with both parents, grandparents and other key family members, we recognised that each family situation is unique and that it is not the conciliator's role to prescribe solutions.

Many parents – and their solicitors – saw the need for a forum allowing confidential discussions of private family matters. Parents were reassured that BCFCS conciliators had no statutory powers to intervene over their children and that discussions that took place during conciliation were not reportable to the courts, neither by conciliators, nor by either party, nor by their legal representatives (unless both parties gave their joint consent, which was unlikely in litigated matters).[2] The courts upheld the legal privilege established in case-law to protect the confidentiality of discussions to explore possibilities of reconciliation and, by extension, conciliation.

Key principles of family conciliation and mediation – that parental responsibility is not ended by divorce, that parents should make their own arrangements for their children as far as possible, without unnecessary interventions by statutory agencies and the courts, and that parents should be encouraged to consider their children's needs – are entirely consistent with the principles of the Children Act 1989, with its emphasis on private ordering by parents and the 'no order' presumption and encouragement to parents to reach joint decisions about arrangements for their children. The Law Commission had considered whether the court should follow this 'minimalist approach' and had referred to the work of conciliators in the review of child custody law that led to the Children Act 1989.[3]

Conciliation in-court and out-of-court – complementary developments

On 15 September 1976 the Presiding Judge of the Western Circuit, Sir Robin Dunn, called a meeting of county court registrars to consider ways of reducing the number of defended divorces set down for a High Court hearing. This led to an in-court conciliation procedure being set up in 1977 by county court registrars in Bristol, using divorce court welfare officers to provide 'in-court conciliation'. Initially limited to defended divorce cases, the procedure was extended in 1978–79

---

[1]   (Finer) *Report of the Committee on One Parent Families* (1974), at para 4.288.
[2]   D Parker and L Parkinson, 'Solicitors and Family Conciliation Services – A Basis for Professional Co-operation' (1985) *Fam Law* 15 at 270.
[3]   Law Commission Working Paper No 96 *Review of Child Law: Custody* (1986), at p 115.

to contested applications over children, when 27 contested custody and access cases were selected for an in-court conciliation appointment.[1] These appointments, like conciliation at BCFCS, had the protection of legal privilege but as they were presided over by a county court registrar and the court welfare officers who staffed them were officers of the court, this inevitably associated in-court conciliation with the court's formal authority. The parties' solicitors attended and spoke on behalf of their clients, who might have a brief discussion with a court welfare officer acting as a conciliator.

It has been suggested that the distinction between in-court and out-of-court conciliation caused unhelpful divisions and that Avon Probation Service was not supportive of BCFCS. In fact, we had great support from senior probation officers, including the Senior Divorce Court Welfare Officer who was married to one of our conciliators! The two services were complementary, offering different forms of settlement-seeking help at different stages in legal proceedings. BCFCS and the Divorce Court Welfare Service worked out referral systems that would avoid the problem of couples in dispute being referred to both services simultaneously.[2] None of us saw conciliation as a universal panacea and it was obvious that not all disputes and not all circumstances would be suitable for conciliation. The willingness of both parents to take part in conciliation discussions, without experiencing fear or pressure, was seen as fundamental.

Referrals to BCFCS from solicitors, the central Citizens' Advice Bureau and parents themselves increased to as many as six per day. One day we received 15 referrals. When conciliation appeared to be suitable and one parent was willing to accept it, a carefully planned approach to the other parent produced a positive response in most cases. By 1981–82, BCFCS was able to demonstrate substantial growth, from about 180 conciliations in 1979–80 to 350 in 1981–82, defined as cases in which both parents attended one or more conciliation sessions. 112 firms of solicitors initiated or concurred with these referrals.[3]

Access to children by the non-resident parent was the issue most frequently referred. An increasing number of referrals involved ambivalence and disagreement over the divorce itself. We found that :

> 'conciliation is accepted by many individuals who rule out reconciliation and refuse marriage guidance counselling ... some of them nonetheless have second thoughts about divorce in the course of conciliation. This change is not due to pressure from the conciliator but to the increased ability of both partners to listen and respond to each other. Early and skilled intervention is essential, preferably before a petition is filed and served.... Couples who stop divorce proceedings in order to attempt reconciliation are usually referred to counselling. Approximately one in six cases changed direction from conciliation to reconciliation in 1981.'[4]

---

[1]   G Parmiter, 'Bristol In-Court Conciliation Procedure' (*Law Society Gazette*, 25.2.81), at p 196.
[2]   BCFCS application to the Nuffield Foundation, 1978, unpublished.
[3]   L Parkinson, *Conciliation in Separation and Divorce* (Croom Helm, 1986), at p 79.
[4]   L Parkinson, 'Conciliation – Pros and Cons' [1983] *Fam Law* 13 at 22.

As well as the increasing number of conciliations, BCFCS received many requests for information, visits and participation at conferences. We received visits from an eminent Japanese professor of family law and from court counsellors working in the Family Court of Australia. There were articles in the local and national press, radio and TV programmes. 'Multi-tasking', if the term existed then, would have been a euphemism for the barrage of enquiries and urgent requests that surged in daily.

Theoretical frameworks for family mediation

In the early years of BCFCS, we were unaware of the work of American mediators such as Coogler[1] and Haynes,[2] whose approach was primarily settlement-directed and who became extremely influential in the development of mediation in the UK and internationally. The Family Conciliation Bureau at Bromley, operating under the wing of South East London Probation Service, followed the structured model of negotiations developed by Coogler, whereas conciliation discussions at BCFCS were more free-ranging. We sought to acknowledge feelings and gave time to discussion of family relationships. The settlement-seeking model of mediation[3] was designed to deal with civil and commercial issues, rather than with child-related issues. The BCFCS model of conciliation owed a great deal to family systems theory and understanding of family processes.[4]

Engaging both partners in a failing or failed marital relationship in face-to-face meetings, to discuss their continuing parental responsibilities and co-operation as parents, is no easy task. Managing joint discussions about practical arrangements, following separation or divorce, and family re-organisation was a new form of professional practice in the 1970s. If only one partner is seen, 'rationalisations too often replace reality, distortions are difficult to challenge, and family transactions cannot be observed'[5]. Our focus was :

> 'the immediate practical needs and emotional interaction of separating or separated couples and their children. Children may be inarticulate, through their age or anxiety, or both, standing silently by while their familiar world disintegrates in fragments of unexplained events. The conciliator helps parents to understand and respond to their children's needs, so that solutions can be worked out which accommodate, as far as possible, the mutual and conflicting needs of adults and children. There is often an additional aim to foster and maintain links between children and grandparents.'[6]

---

[1]   G Davis and M Roberts, *Access to Agreement* (Open University Press, 1988), at p 14; OJ Coogler, *Structured Mediation in Divorce Settlement* (Lexington Books, 1978).

[2]   J Haynes, *Divorce Mediation* (Springer Publishing Company, 1981).

[3]   R Fisher and W Ury, *Getting to Yes – Negotiating Agreement Without Giving In* (Houghton-Mifflin, 1981).

[4]   B Paolucci et al, *Family Decision-Making – An Eco-system Approach* (John Wiley, 1977).

[5]   J Steinberg 'Towards an Interdisciplinary Commitment' (1980) *Journal of Marital and Family Therapy*, at p 259.

[6]   L Parkinson, 'Conciliation: A New Approach to Family Conflict Resolution' (1982) *British Journal of Social Work* 13, at p 22.

Conflict theory[1] encourages acceptance of conflict as a natural force that can be harnessed in the management of change, depending on whether the energy is used constructively or destructively. This view rejects the stigmatising notion that conflict implies pathology and that divorcing couples need therapy. The conciliation client 'remains the subject of rights, not the object of assistance'.[2] Couples who came to conciliation were encouraged to listen to and respect each other's point of view, to understand and evaluate the options available to them and to reach their own, considered decisions.

One of the main difficulties is that separating and divorcing couples are usually at very different stages of emotional and psychological adjustment. This generally begins much earlier for the leaver than for the left partner. A partner who is abandoned is left behind emotionally, as well as physically. Acute feelings of shock, rejection and betrayal often spill over on to children and financial issues. Although many parents come to mediation in an emotionally fragile state, they are expected to negotiate over arrangements for their children and financial matters in a reasonable way, at a time when their ability to think rationally may be temporarily diminished. When decisions are needed on many different issues simultaneously, it is hardly surprising that many people feel overwhelmed. Outrage and anger can quickly spread from one issue to another. On the other hand, co-operation and agreement in one area help to maintain trust and increase co-operation in other areas. A dialogue is needed – but many separating or separated couples find this dialogue very hard to manage on their own. Mediators need to be able to adapt their approach and pace, responding to different reactions to conflict and the different stage each partner may be at in their emotional and psychological divorce.

Crisis theory[3] is relevant to conciliation in suggesting that crisis involves risks, but also offers opportunities for positive growth and change. This positive view of crisis emphasises the need for relevant information and good communication, to help family members cope with changes in every dimension of their lives, without succumbing to depression or despair. Professor Caplan showed a personal interest in the work of BCFCS, since crisis intervention strategies are fundamental in conciliation. It is important to recognise that the acute emotional turmoil experienced during relationship breakdown is normal, not abnormal. It may also be possible for conciliators to anticipate and possibly pre-empt further crises that may occur, for example when a parent hands over the children to the other parent.

Continuing funding crises in the 1980s

Many of those who championed the conciliation cause based their case on the savings in legal aid and court costs that would be achieved through conciliation. BCFCS stressed the importance of family autonomy and privacy, of helping parents to reach joint decisions for the benefit of their children and to develop an

---

[1]   M Deutsch, *The Resolution of Conflict* (Yale University Press, 1973).

[2]   Finer Report (1974), at para 4 285.

[3]   G Caplan, *A Community Approach to Mental Health* (Tavistock, 1961); H Parad, *Crisis Intervention* (Family Service Association of America, 1965).

innovative model of participative decision-making. The Lord Chancellor's Legal Aid Advisory Committee recommended support for BCFCS on three grounds:

'First and foremost we consider that anything that can reduce conflict and bitterness when marriage fails is to the advantage of any children who may be involved. Secondly it might prove to be a method of keeping down unnecessary legal costs and demands on the courts. Thirdly it seems to be pioneering new forms of collaboration between solicitors and social workers within the jurisdiction of family law.... We hope that this worthwhile project will not fail through want of further funds.'[1]

One of the main obstacles in seeking government funding was that responsibilities for legal aid, courts administration and the Divorce Court Welfare Service were divided between the Lord Chancellor's Department (LCD) and the Home Office. Urgent appeals from BCFCS were batted like a ping-pong ball between the LCD and the Home Office, with occasional encouraging pats from the Secretary of State for Health and Social Security, who saw possible benefits for one-parent families and in reducing the numbers of children taken into care under matrimonial care orders. The Treasury, on the other hand, wanted convincing evidence of savings to the public purse, before it would approve any funding at all.

In May 1980, when the continuation of the Nuffield grant in the second year hung in the balance and BCFCS was on the brink of closure, the Lord Chancellor's Department came up with a partial solution: a disbursement of £20 would be payable for conciliation under the 'Green Form' scheme, in cases where the client was being advised by a solicitor under this scheme or was in receipt of legal aid. The disbursement could not be paid direct to BCFCS: the service had to invoice the legal adviser and send reminders in many cases, since solicitors' Green Form and legal aid claims were submitted on completion of their work, long after conciliation had finished. These driblets of public funding for conciliation were totally unsatisfactory, raising only a small proportion of the funds needed. Most of it was spent on administrative work to collect the payments.

In 1981, when crisis time came round again, the Lord Chancellor's Legal Aid Advisory Committee warned that it was 'imperative' that BCFCS should not close through lack of funds:

'It would be extremely short-sighted for a Service which not only provides a more satisfactory way of resolving disputes but may well also save money ... to be forced to close before it reaches the end of its experimental period.'[2]

While BCFCS engaged in its annual struggle for continuing funding, the Council of Bristol Law Society passed a resolution that 'the termination of BCFCS would be detrimental to the public, the legal profession, and to the work of the courts in family matters'.[3] In conveying this resolution to the Lord Chancellor's Department

---

[1]   Lord Chancellor's Advisory Committee on Legal Aid *29th Legal Aid Annual Reports 1978–79* (HMSO, 1979), at para 57.

[2]   Lord Chancellor's Advisory Committee on Legal Aid *30th Annual Reports 1979–80* (HMSO, 1981), at para 58.

[3]   J Westcott, Private correspondence.

in support of the service's plea for financial support, the President of Bristol Law Society wrote:

> 'To my mind, BCFCS is much more than another piece of social work. Its principal achievement, I believe, is to demonstrate that an informal system of conciliation can work in harmony with a judicial system, the one complementing and supporting the other. In my view, this achievement may well show a direction in which a reform of the whole family law system might proceed.'

A year later, the Lord Chancellor's Legal Aid Advisory Committee wrote:

> 'As we said last year, we believe that a decision is long overdue on how such initiatives should be directed and funded. We continue to believe that the development and extension of appropriate conciliation arrangements and their incorporation as far as possible into matrimonial procedure are vitally important measures necessary to reduce the expense of litigation in this area and the amount of unhappiness which at present results from it.'[1]

Those who imagine that a pioneer service could obtain funding more easily than services set up later have no idea of the struggles we had. Support came from many quarters – from the National Council for One Parent Families, the Legal Aid Group, the Archbishop of Canterbury, the All Party Parliamentary Group for Children, the President of the Family Division of the High Court, High Court and county court judges, academics, the Probation Service, the British Association of Social Workers, the National Association of Citizens' Advice Bureaux, the National Marriage Guidance Council, Families Need Fathers and many others. Organisations such as Marriage Guidance and the Catholic Marriage Advisory Council which might have been in competition for funding or who might have misperceived conciliation as promoting divorce, nonetheless supported us.

An official from the Lord Chancellor's Department who came to visit BCFCS expressed the hope that conciliators would work as unpaid volunteers. He made the mistake of calling us 'you nice charitable ladies'. He received the sharp response that we were definitely not charitable and possibly not ladies. The government's response to widespread pressure to fund conciliation was to set up an Inter-departmental Committee on Conciliation, made up of civil servants from six government departments :

> 'to review current arrangements for conciliation
>
> (a) to report on the nature, scope and effects of existing facilities and services;
> (b) to consider whether those or further facilities should be promoted and developed within existing resource planning; and
> (c) to consider any consequential changes in matrimonial law or procedure.'[2]

An official in the Lord Chancellor's Department commented in private that the cost of setting up the Interdepartmental Committee and producing its report would have

---

[1]   Lord Chancellor's Advisory Committee on Legal Aid *32nd Annual Reports* 1981–82 (HMSO, 1981), at para 105.
[2]   Inter-Departmental Committee on Conciliation *Report* (HMSO, 1983), at para 1.1.

funded pioneer family conciliation services for a considerable time. Unfortunately the method used by the Committee's researchers to assess the effectiveness of out-of-court conciliation was to compare cases referred to conciliation with divorce court files. Only divorces where the court file showed that agreement on ancillary matters had been reached through conciliation were counted as 'successful conciliations'. In many BCFCS conciliations, there was no divorce and no court file. Some couples reached separation agreements, some wished to delay their divorce until after 2 years' separation, some were unmarried and others moved from conciliation to marital counselling. In all these cases, the Interdepartmental Committee regarded conciliation as 'failed'. A thousand pages of quantifiable data assembled by the BCFCS co-ordinator were returned to the service after 4 days, clearly unread. On the basis of their questionable assessment, the Inter-departmental Committee concluded that out-of-court conciliation did not save costs overall and that conciliation would be better provided by court-based services and court procedures ... and that further research should be commissioned before any policy decisions were taken.

The furore over the Inter-departmental Committee's Report led to the Lord Chancellor's Department setting up a Conciliation Project Unit at the University of Newcastle-upon-Tyne. The Project Unit researchers undertook a nationwide survey of divorce courts and conciliation services, selecting six independent, out-of-court services and 10 court-based services for detailed study. Meanwhile, the pressure to manage the day-to-day running of the service, write reports, publicise the service and make continuous bids for funding, while at the same time conciliating and developing the process and practice of conciliation, was very heavy and took its toll.

The origins of the National Family Conciliation Council (NFCC, later NFM)

The idea of setting up a national association of independent family conciliation services to share experience, to draw up standards of practice for family conciliation and to combine forces in the campaign for public funding, originated at a meeting in Bristol in October 1978 between two divorce court welfare officers from Surrey and the co-ordinator of BCFCS. When enough projects were underway for a national association to be viable, the BCFCS co-ordinator convened a meeting in London. This meeting on 16 January 1981 was attended by representatives of 11 services (with apologies from three others) and was chaired by a senior probation officer who was also Chairman of Leeds Marriage Guidance Council. The 11 representatives of new or proposed conciliation schemes included a Chief Probation Officer, four Assistant Chief Probation Officers, two senior divorce court welfare officers, the secretary to Manchester Legal Services Committee and social workers representing three other independent services. A brief statement from each member of the group revealed that each area was at a different stage of development and proceeding on rather different lines, some relying on their local Probation Service or National Marriage Guidance to provide accommodation and administrative back-up, whereas others were setting up independent services. We agreed a common definition of conciliation as 'helping separating and divorcing couples to reach agreed decisions on matters arising from the breakdown of their marriage, especially matters concerning children'.[1] By the time of the second meeting in April 1981, we were aware of 24 operational or projected schemes. The national association became known as the National Family Conciliation Council (NFCC). At the first national conference in Birmingham in October 1982 a steering committee was elected and given the tasks of drafting a constitution, drawing up criteria for affiliation, preparing a training programme for conciliators and applying for charitable status. A Code of Practice for Family Conciliation Services was drafted in consultation with the Law Society's Family Law Committee.[2] Family lawyers continued to give support from the sidelines and became increasingly interested in joining in.

All issues mediation and interdisciplinary co-mediation, 1985

Experience had shown the limitations of mediating about children without full exploration of inter-related financial and property issues. In 1985 a pilot project was launched to provide mediation on all issues, including finance and property, using a co-mediation model in which a family mediator from a social work/family therapy background co-mediated with a mediator from a legal background.[3] This proposal was put to NFCC conciliators through the NFCC newsletter[4] but NFCC preferred at that time to maintain its prime focus on child-related issues.

The six founder members of 'Solicitors in Mediation', as the project was called (despite being interdisciplinary), approached the Law Society. A joint working party was set up by the Law Society's family law committee and after 18 months the Law Society changed its professional practice rules to permit solicitors to act as mediators in a separate professional role, outside their legal practice. The rule was later amended to allow solicitors to offer mediation within their legal practice.[5]

The members of the pilot project drew up a code of practice and documents for all issues mediation – referral forms, the Agreement to Mediate, a financial questionnaire (referred to when 'Form E' was drafted) and precedents for mediation summaries.[6] An article in *The Times* led to over a hundred referrals for all-issues mediation during the pilot scheme from 1986–88. Increasing interest in all-issues mediation and interdisciplinary co-mediation led to the setting up of the Family Mediators Association (FMA) in December 1988. Representatives of NFCC, the Institute of Family Therapy, Relate, the Family Law Bar Association and the Probation Service were invited to join an advisory committee so that different forms of mediation would evolve in complementary ways. A 2-year grant was obtained from the Nuffield Foundation to develop training for mediation on all issues. The first training course was run in June 1989 and two more courses were run later that year. Many family lawyers, social workers, counsellors and conciliators became enthusiastic about the model of interdisciplinary co-mediation.

[1]   National Family Conciliation Council, minutes of 1st meeting, 16.1.81.
[2]   National Family Conciliation Council Code of Practice [1984] *Fam Law* 14 at 107.
[3]   L Parkinson, 'Co-Mediation with a Lawyer Mediator' [1989] *Fam Law* 48 at 48 and 135.
[4]   L Parkinson, *Conciliation* (the Newsletter of the National Family Conciliation Council No 14 August 1986), at p 19.
[5]   H Brown and A Marriott, *ADR Principles and Practice* (Sweet & Maxwell, 1993), at p 335.
[6]   L Parkinson, *Family Mediation* (Sweet & Maxwell, 1997).

FMA's advisory group became a Family Mediation Forum which met regularly and produced working papers and joint recommendations to the Lord Chancellor's Department. The Forum worked co-operatively – a fact that was often overlooked in reports of mediation bodies competing with each other. We believed that

> 'while the organisation and funding of conciliation and mediation services are public policy issues ..., practice and standards of practice need to be held in joint, rather than sole, custody by the professionals involved in this field.'[1]

The researchers in the Conciliation Project Unit found that the wider scope of all-issues mediation contributed to settlement and that lawyer mediators made a significant contribution. All-issues mediation achieved good results in 'improving communication between couples, reducing bitterness and tension, clarifying areas of disagreement and enabling couples to negotiate'.[2] These findings encouraged NFCC (later National Family Mediation) to develop mediation on all issues, using lawyers as consultants to the conciliators, rather than as co-mediators.

The development of family mediation in Europe

International conferences on family mediation brought Australian and North American mediators to London in 1984 and 1986. In 1990 the first European conference on family mediation was held in France and this led to family mediation trainers from several European countries meeting to formulate standards for family mediation training. A series of meetings held in Paris, Geneva and Brussels resulted in the publication in 1992 of a European Charter on Training in Family Mediation, in French and English.

In 1998 the Council of Europe's Committee of experts on family law recognised the need for an international directive on family mediation:

> 'Research in Europe, North America, Australia and New Zealand suggests that family mediation is better suited than more formal legal mechanisms to the settlement of sensitive, emotional issues surrounding family matters. Reaching agreements in mediation has been shown to be a vital component in making and maintaining co-operative relationships between divorcing parents: it reduces conflict and encourages continuing contact between children and both their parents.'[3]

Their recommendation was formally adopted by the Committee of Ministers of the Council of Europe:

> 'Realising that a number of States are considering the introduction of family mediation (and) convinced of the need to make greater use of family mediation, [the Council of Europe] recommends the governments of member States:
>
> i. to introduce or promote family mediation, or, where necessary, strengthen existing family mediation;

---

[1] L Parkinson in T Fisher (ed) *Family Conciliation within the UK* (Jordans, 1990), at p 142.

[2] Walker, McCarthy and Timms, *Mediation: the Making and Remaking of Co-operative Relationships* (Relate Centre for Family Studies, University of Newcastle, 1994), at p 80.

[3] Council of Europe *Recommendation No R (98) 1* 21 January 1998, at para 7.

ii.   to take or reinforce all measures they consider necessary with a view to the implementation of the following principles for the promotion and use of family mediation as an appropriate means of resolving family disputes.'[1]

When couples are ending their marriage or partnership, they need a bridge to make the transition to new or renegotiated family arrangements and relationships. It is the mediator's task to provide a bridge for them, to enable them to survey their territory and map out a route that both of them consider manageable, for themselves and for their children.

In England and Wales, the Family Law Act 1996 was a mile-stone in the history of family mediation, providing public funding for those eligible via a system of referrals to recognised family mediators, so that those seeking legal aid for family proceedings could consider the suitability of mediation as an alternative to litigation.[2] In 2002/2003, 13,841 publicly funded family mediations were started, an increase of 12 per cent over the previous year; 21,146 clients who took part in mediation received it free of charge – an increase of 14 per cent; 74 per cent of all publicly funded mediations (family and non-family) were resolved without recourse to the courts.[3]

Family mediation has developed rapidly across Europe in recent years, although the level of organisation varies a great deal and few other countries have quality assurance systems regulating mediation training and practice.[4] With the increasing mobility of people across Europe, mediation is needed to resolve disputes over children that involve an international element. Mediation is also used in schools and in many other spheres. From an early age, children need to learn ways of managing arguments and settling disagreements in constructive ways.

Recently, two parents who were taking part in mediation told me that their 6-year-old daughter and a boy in her class had been chosen by their classmates to act as mediators in settling classroom disagreements and differences. Children under-stand mediation very well. Now even a 6-year-old can become a mediator.

---

[1]   Council of Europe *Recommendation No. R (98) 1* 21 January 1998, at para 7.
[2]   Family Law Act 1996, Part III Mediation.
[3]   Legal Services Commission Statistics 2002/2003.
[4]   L Parkinson, *Family Mediation in Europe*, paper given to the European Masters in Mediation course, Sion, Switzerland, March 2003.

Chapter 4

THE RESPONSE OF THE LEGAL PROFESSION

David Woodward

Climate for the practice of Family Law in the 1970s

In the early 1970s, solicitors were coming to terms with the implementation of the Divorce Reform Act 1969, the so-called 'Casanova's Charter', a description which arose from the new ground of divorce following 5 years of separation without consent. Undefended divorce cases were held in open court when the petitioner (normally the wife) had to give evidence to prove her case. She also had to satisfy the judge about the arrangements for the care of the children. He would then make Custody and Access Orders. In these circumstances, my first duty as an Articled Clerk was to provide a tissue to dry the eye of the wife at her undefended divorce hearing. Generally, however, my responsibility was to ensure an uninterrupted flow of cases for my principal, who could have up to 10 consecutive hearings in a morning.

As well as solicitors, hard-nosed legal executives also plied their trade in the field of matrimonial advice. They were very experienced and seemed to play a hard tactical game, treating custody and access disputes like any other piece of litigation. Divorce pleadings were full of red and green amendments and suitably bound in coloured tape. A custody dispute would procedurally resemble a running down action. In those days, solicitors did not consider co-operation between lawyers. They did not seek solutions for their clients but sought to win a contest. The adversarial system reigned supreme. There was no formal organisation of family lawyers such as the Solicitors Family Law Association, with a willingness to find solutions for clients. Instead, battle lines were drawn and the legal fog of war prevailed, just as dense cigarette smoke always polluted the waiting rooms and corridors of the courts.

In the 1970s, matrimonial law was a lucrative and expanding area of practice for solicitors. Divorce petitions doubled between 1970 and 1976 from 70,575 to 143,465. In 1977 alone, 200,000 children were involved in divorce. In 1978/79, £30m was spent on legal aid for matrimonial proceedings, which represented 75 per cent of the Civil Legal Aid expenditure. Most, if not all, firms offered matrimonial advice at that time. It is probably true to say that a significant proportion of solicitors were keen to protect their family law practices and reluctant to contemplate any new schemes which might disrupt the status quo.

Family law climate in Bristol in the 1970s

Nevertheless, some Bristol solicitors felt the need for a 'better way' as a means of improving on the old adversarial system. Their thoughts were stimulated and focused by the publication of the Finer Report in 1974, which led to a Bristol Conference which Professor Murch has described. Indeed, Bristol soon proved a fertile ground in which the search for innovative ways of conducting matrimonial litigation could be developed. It is of note that these local discussions seeking a collaborative approach to family law took place prior to the setting up nationally of the Solicitors Family Law Association in December 1982.

The influence of the Bristol judges in general and of registrars in particular was crucial, although in the initial stages enthusiasm was not unanimous. The senior Registrar, Geoffrey Parmiter, was notably committed to a 'better way' and was highly influential in achieving progress in this area. Furthermore, it is certainly true that the 1970s and early 1980s produced in Bristol a substantial number of newly qualified solicitors who were noticeably forward-looking and receptive to new ideas, though it is unclear whether this was the cause or effect of the emergence of a conciliation service in the city.

The ground may have been fertile but a substantial amount of cultivation was undoubtedly needed, if new ideas and practices were to take root. In the Council of the Bristol Law Society at that time two somewhat unhelpful views were expressed. First, that the Council had a duty to protect the work of its members against interlopers, ie conciliators who were trespassing onto their 'patch'. Secondly, once a solicitor had accepted instructions from a client in divorce, it was his or her duty to remain responsible to that client throughout and it would, therefore, be wrong to transfer any of that responsibility to a third party, especially one outside the legal profession. At the Bristol Family Law Conference held on 19 March 1982, a local solicitor claimed, 'the duty of a solicitor is to act in the best interest of his client within the rules of the court. If the rules encourage a solicitor to be pugnacious, then don't blame the solicitor. Change the rules to change the approach of the solicitor'. He and other members of the old guard still saw the court as the solicitor's sole preserve. With attitudes such as these still being quite widely, and perhaps understandably, held, it is clear that there was considerable work to be done before a conciliation service could hope to operate effectively in Bristol.

Bristol solicitors' requirements of the BCFCS

Local solicitors had very specific requirements if the proposed BCFCS was to gain their support. Solicitors had to be satisfied that discussions within conciliation were confidential and legally privileged, the latter being an extremely important issue to them. Solicitors were exceedingly nervous of the possibility that their client's discussions or concessions might be reported to the court. The BCFCS obtained Counsel's opinion, which the courts endorsed, that discussions were privileged, thereby answering solicitors' concerns. It remains, however, a sensitive area and 25 years on it is still occasionally necessary to make applications to exclude privileged material which has been erroneously included in open documents.

Another area for concern amongst local solicitors at that time was that of the qualifications and training of the conciliators. Solicitors needed assurance of the competence and training of those to whom they were referring their clients. The solicitors insisted upon an assurance that no legal advice would be given to their clients, that conciliators would not deal with financial matters and that there would be no cost to the client. Solicitors were understandably anxious not to hand over their practice to conciliators and did not wish to give their clients a choice between paying the conciliator or paying the solicitor. Finally, of course, if the solicitor was prepared to refer a client to conciliation, he expected the service to offer an immediate appointment.

How the BCFCS worked with lawyers

In order to develop, the service obviously needed the co-operation of supportive Bristol solicitors. Despite the reservations described above, there were positive signs in the shape of that fertile ground which has already been mentioned. Consequently, Lisa Parkinson targeted a number of the more enlightened solicitors to encourage them to refer clients and to share her evangelical approach. She had one-to-one meetings with solicitors, as well as larger open meetings to explain conciliation, deal with misconceptions and answer questions. These dialogues were generally well received, developing interest among practitioners and paving the way to their involvement in conciliation.

Acceptance of the BCFCS was greatly assisted by judicial and court welfare officers' support. By the early 1980s, judicial support extended beyond Bristol. Indeed, in 1983 the President of the Family Division, Sir John Arnold, wrote in *Family Law*:

> 'In very many cases the questions which arise in relation to the upbringing of the children and the financial and property arrangements between spouses are resolved by agreement. In very many other cases, however, they have to be fought out in an adversarial system of litigation. This can be, and very often is a bruising experience from which both parties emerge with varying degrees of bitterness and resentment. The consequential attitudes very frequently affect the children and in particular their relationships with their parents. The damage which is inflicted on the individuals concerned takes its toll in delinquency and ill health.'

Referring to the Lord Chancellor's Inter-Departmental Committee, he added that its findings were awaited,

> 'with the greatest interest and it is greatly to be hoped that we are on the threshold of important developments which cannot be other than highly beneficial to the community as well as involving, as is widely believed, a significant saving in public expenditure.'

The President's interest in conciliation in general and the BCFCS in particular added considerable impetus to the development of the service.

In a further development, Bristol Registrars introduced a pre-trial review procedure and began to refer cases directly to conciliation. The circuit judges were known, on occasions, to refer injunction cases direct to conciliation. Now that solicitors could see a bandwagon starting to roll, many opted to jump aboard, recognising the benefits to be derived from participating in the new service. Not all were entirely positive in their approach, however. Some chose to refer their most difficult cases in the expectation, and maybe the hope, that conciliation would fail. It is also certainly true that there were solicitors at that time who would express relief at being able to offload their particularly intractable access disputes onto the service. Despite the possibly suspect motives of such practitioners, the BCFCS was beginning to gain impetus in the local legal world, gradually convincing Bristol solicitors of its potential to achieve solutions even in the most difficult of circumstances.

How the BCFCS worked in practice

The BCFCS leaflet distributed in September 1980 explained the service on offer in the following way:

> **'A CONFIDENTIAL SERVICE FOR SEPARATING OR DIVORCING COUPLES AND THEIR CHILDREN**
>
> THE BRISTOL COURTS FAMILY CONCILIATION SERVICE helps separating or divorcing couples to settle disputes, especially over children, and to co-operate with each other as parents. Confidential and informal discussion assists them to work out acceptable arrangements in relation to custody, access and the occupation of the matrimonial home.
>
> Although conciliation does not rule out the possibility of reconciliation, it is mainly concerned with people who are ending their marriage/relationship. It can help them to sort out their affairs with as little anger and distress as possible.
>
> Referrals to the service are usually made by solicitors, who continue to give any legal and financial advice that may be necessary. However, people can also approach us direct (by letter, telephone, or personal visit). Couples are offered separate or joint appointments, depending on the situation. No report is made to the Court or to any other agency. The service is staffed by qualified conciliators who have specialist training in this work.'

When separating or divorcing couples showed an interest in the BCFCS, either solicitors completed a referral form or there were self-referrals in some circumstances. Between May 1979 and August 1980, 65 Bristol firms made 360 referrals to the service, while 10 firms agreed to self-referrals. Of those 65 firms, one provided 44 referrals, one firm 17 referrals and 9 firms between 11 and 15 referrals. These figures show that in the first 16 months of its existence, the BCFCS was already having an impact on a significant number of cases in the city.

Funding remained problematic, however. If the client was eligible under a Green Form or legal aid certificate, the solicitor could claim a fee for completing the referral form and the BCFCS would bill the solicitor £20, which he would then claim on his consolidated Green Form claims form or his Bill for Taxation. Solicitors often stored up Green Form claims for many months and taxation was completed after several years of litigation, so payment to the BCFCS was very slow and erratic, leading to a significant number of bad debts. This did not help develop a good relationship between solicitors and the service. The £20 was certainly hopeless as a sustainable source of funding. In 1982, Lisa Parkinson wrote in *Family Law*:

> 'The total cost of running BCFCS for one year is equivalent to the average cost of legal aid for both parties (assuming both are legally aided) for 30 contested matrimonial cases in the High Court or County Court (i.e. contested issues; in an acrimonious divorce there may be several contested issues which are the subject of separate applications to the court). BCFCS is currently undertaking conciliation in over 300 cases annually.
>
> The financial and social costs of matrimonial disputes are extremely high, and expenditure on civil legal aid has increased both in the number of matrimonial proceedings and in the average costs per case. Under the 'Green Form' a Petitioner on a low income can obtain a divorce for less than the cost of a marriage certificate. Marriage certificates are not subsidised by the state. One possible way of funding conciliation services could perhaps be to introduce a new charge on the Decree Absolute, for which either the Petitioner or the Respondent is able to apply. The Applicant is likely to be the party most anxious to remarry. Funds collected at the end of the divorce process could be allocated to approved conciliation schemes which can demonstrate their ability to resolve at least some of the disputes which arise at the beginning of the divorce process.'

These financial difficulties have always remained a problem to the service and are described in greater detail by Trevor Morkham in Chapter 9.

As time passed and the service proved itself, opposition from the more die-hard local solicitors gradually diminished and eventually evaporated for four reasons. First, the general public supported the principle of conciliation. Secondly, solicitors found they could trust the skill and professionalism of the conciliators. Thirdly, the service was introducing new clients to those solicitors who supported it. Fourthly, and perhaps most importantly, solicitors came to see the advantage to their clients and to their practice of not only embracing conciliation, but also influencing its development.

Lawyer mediators

Solicitors in Mediation began in London in February 1986 and led to a Code of Practice prepared by a joint working party representing the Law Society, the Family Law Committee, the SFLA and members of the pilot scheme. This Code of Practice opened the door to lawyers to train as mediators, reassured that they were not in breach of professional conduct rules. With the BCFCS well established in Bristol, lawyers in the City were encouraged to become lawyer mediators. The decision to become involved in mediation in this way was often motivated by the desire to gain a better understanding of the client's feelings about and experiences of separation. At the same time, there was an enthusiasm to learn a most worthwhile new skill. I myself was sufficiently enthused by the training to put mediation into practice, which I continue to do.

There has been much development involving co-mediation, all issues medi-ation and public funding for mediation, all of which is covered in detail by Thelma Fisher in Chapter 7. As far as Bristol is concerned, the practice of mediation by solicitors is now as commonplace a part of the solicitor's skills as smoking in court corridors and defended divorces are now the exception.

Bristol Family Mediation in 2004

In 25 years, mediation has become an integral part of family lawyers' practice in Bristol. Solicitors who have qualified in the last 10 years know of nothing different; indeed, it is now good practice to consider mediation at the first meeting with the client.

For publicly funded clients, mediation is the gateway to funding. The development of mediation practices has been based on publicly funded contracts. This is a far cry from the Green Form allowance of £20 per client in the 1980s. The linking of public funding to mediation now reflects the status of today's professional mediation services.

The client now has a choice of models, of mediation and of mediation suppliers. These include co-mediation, sole mediation, sole mediation with a lawyer mediator involvement at a later stage, not-for-profit suppliers, solicitor consortium suppliers, suppliers who see children and those who do not.

While separating and divorcing couples today enjoy the benefits of the mediation service with the full support of their solicitors, there is a certain irony seeing solicitors now compete with BFM for mediation, when in the 1970s and early 1980s many were reluctant to allow their clients to participate in mediation at all.

Chapter 5

THE RESPONSE FROM THE COURTS

District Judge Roger Bird

Introduction

This chapter has to begin on a personal note. I remember well the Bristol Finer meeting and the meeting at Bristol University in 1974 which led to the setting up of the Bristol Conciliation Service and then, eventually, to the new system of preliminary hearings in children cases. This chapter is concerned only with the way in which the procedure of the Bristol County Court changed as a result of the new ideas.

The senior circuit judge in Bristol then was Harry Russell, who was always very supportive of the new ideas, but the prime mover among the judiciary was Geoffrey Parmiter, then senior registrar (later district judge) at the Bristol County Court. I think it is fair to say that the success of the new scheme which came about as a result of the meetings was very largely due to Geoffrey's enthusiasm and dedication. When I became a registrar in 1979 and attended circuit meetings for the first time, it was noticeable that, to put it mildly, not all Geoffrey's colleagues shared his enthusiasm for mediation and some were openly hostile. The position is now completely different. As will be seen below, the 'Bristol scheme', or something very like it, is now the norm, and the struggles which Geoffrey endured 25 years ago would now be unthinkable.

The Bristol scheme

Before the changes which began in relation to defended divorces in 1976 and were extended locally to children's cases in 1978 the court procedure for dealing with an application for what would now be called a section 8 order (residence, contact, specific issue or prohibited steps) was haphazard and unpredictable. If one was lucky, someone, either circuit judge or registrar, held a directions appointment before the final hearing. A welfare report would be ordered. Eventually the case would get to trial. There was no real case-management and certainly no attempt to find a mediated solution.

The Bristol scheme changed all this. All cases were given a first appointment before the registrar who sat with a duty court welfare officer. In those cases which were not resolved immediately, the parties were invited to go to another room with the welfare officer who would discuss some of the issues with them and try to help them to reach an agreement. This process might last up to 30 minutes and so could not be much more than emergency first aid, but in about a third of all cases a successful result was achieved and an agreed order made.

Where the issues required further and more detailed consideration a welfare report would be ordered and a final hearing fixed. In some cases the parties might agree to go to the Conciliation Service for a more thorough process of mediation.

This remains essentially the procedure today in Bristol. Various refinements have been introduced. First, a further filtering process now occurs in the form of a pre-trial review 2 weeks after the report is filed and a week or so before the final hearing. About half of the remaining cases either settle at that stage or proceed on only limited issues. At the pre-trial review (PTR) the district judge sits alone and takes the parties through the recommendations (if any) in the report, pointing out that there is Court of Appeal authority for the proposition that, while the report cannot decide the case, a party dissatisfied with the report has to be able to advance some good reason as to why any recommendation should not be accepted; it is not enough merely to disagree with it. (My impression is that the success rate of the PTR has increased since district judges acquired the same jurisdiction to deal with the final hearings as circuit judges.)

The second variation, which was less successful, involved BMS (as it came to be called) itself. Where cases did not respond to the intervention of the duty CWO, the district judge would advise the parties to go for a more thorough-going process of mediation at BMS. He would have the BMS diary there and would be able to offer appointments there and then. The diary would be collected by BMS at the conclusion of every first appointment day.

This scheme eventually was abandoned. BMS probably has its own explanation of why this happened. From the point of view of the court, it was found that fewer people were taking up the offer of mediation. The same number were seeing the duty CWO and the same number of cases was being resolved but it was found that the cases which did not settle there and then were the more intractable ones where a report was definitely needed. Most of those cases had been handled by Bristol solicitors who were very pro-mediation; elsewhere in this book David Woodward explains the effect on the legal profession in Bristol of the 'conciliation movement'. The result was that only the difficult cases got to court and survived the first appointment. In effect, BMS was squeezed out of the process.

The approach of other courts

As indicated in the introduction above, not all courts welcomed the Bristol scheme. An early enthusiast for mediation was the then registrar of the Wandsworth County Court, David Price, who rivalled Geoffrey Parmiter in his proselytising zeal, but many older registrars continued to resist on the ground that they were 'lawyers not social workers'. However, over the next few years attitudes changed, new registrars were appointed with different views, and slowly but surely the spirit of the new system came to pervade the whole country.

In January 1983 the Principal Registry of the Family Division (PRFD) established its own system of conciliation hearings which was subsequently modified in 1991 and again has been recently modified further to provide for children over 11 to attend the conciliation appointment. In a Direction dated 28 July 1986 ([1986] 2 FLR 171) the then senior registrar directed that before ordering a welfare report a judge should, where local conciliation facilities exist, 'consider whether the case is a suitable one for attempts to be made to settle any of the issues by the conciliation process and, if so, a direction to this effect should be included in the order'.

By 1990 there were few, if any, courts in the country that did not operate some form of in court mediation or conciliation. Exactly what form that took is a separate matter which will be considered below.

The Children Act 1989

It will have been seen that, while conciliation was the prime purpose of the Bristol scheme, a secondary but highly important element was case management. Cases were no longer allowed to drift; they received specific timetables and directions from the court which had to be observed.

This element of court direction was one of the most important procedural innovations to be contained in the Children Act 1989, which remains the statute governing law and procedure in this area and which was, at the time, radical and far-reaching. One essential principle of the Act was that delay was not to be permitted in children cases.

It would be going too far to say that the inspiration for these admirable provisions was the Bristol scheme. Nevertheless, it is arguable that, 14 years after the Bristol changes began, the climate of opinion among judges and practitioners had undergone a profound change, and this change must have had some effect on those responsible for the 1989 Act.

What form of conciliation appointment?

Since conciliation became established as one of the most important factors in the first directions appointment, various forms of hearing have sprung up around the country. It has seemed to many people that this is anomalous and that, just as there is now a standard procedure for ancillary relief applications the same should apply to children cases. In the early 1990s, while a member of the Children Act Advisory Committee, I urged the committee and the Family Policy department in the Lord Chancellor's Department, to carry out research with a view to standardising procedure throughout the country. This request fell on deaf ears though, as will be seen below, I was not the first to draw this situation to the attention of the Department. The conventional wisdom was, and to some extent still is, that local conditions vary and that local judges and CAFCASS offices should be free to make their own arrangements.

I recently carried out some fairly basic research into how fellow district judges in England and Wales conduct the first appointments in their courts. I received information from 84 district judges and estimate that they cover more than 50 per cent of the courts dealing with family cases. I classified the types of approach into five categories, as follows:

(a)   Cases where the district judge sits with a CAFCASS officer who is then available in appropriate cases to take the parties away to mediate before returning to the district judge.

(b)   The district judge sits alone and may refer to CAFCASS or a mediation service for mediation at a later date.

(c)   The parties have to see a mediator before the date of the first appointment.

(d)   There is no mediation appointment and if the district judge is unable to resolve the case a CAFCASS report is ordered.

(e)   Some other system.

The results of my research were that my respondents adopt the following systems:

(a)   60%
(b)   12%
(c)   12%
(d)   2%
(e)   14%.

(e) was normally a combination of some of the other systems.

The following points of interest come out of this. First, very few courts have no involvement of a conciliator at or near the first appointment. Secondly, there is still wide variation in practices around the country. The second point is worth exploring a little further, but first I have to record that it has now come to my attention that my predecessor on the Children Act Advisory Committee, District Judge Tony Cleary, performed almost exactly the same research in 1993 and arrived at very similar conclusions. In his report to the Lord Chancellor's Department he commented on the 'lack of uniformity' and 'startling lack of harmony' to be found. He commented that 'there is an overriding impression of ad hoc arrangements which may well have developed both prior and subsequent to the Children Act, based upon the design of one or more enthusiastic supporters of the mediation process who have persuaded particular courts to experiment with their own ideas of "best practice"'.

I can but echo those comments and point out that nothing has changed in 11 years.

It is a strange fact that Part IV of the Family Proceedings Rules which governs children cases does not specify a particular procedure to be followed. Rule 4.14(2) provides that the court 'may' give, vary or revoke directions but imposes no obligation on it to do so. Still less is there any rule dictating what should happen at any directions appointment.

This has led to courts developing their own local procedures as has been seen from the statistics given above. The fact that the practices of courts vary so widely means that practitioners from areas outside a particular court, or even visiting judges, have to enquire as to the method of disposal of cases in that court. This can be time-wasting and confusing and there seems in principle to be no reason for it. One can draw a comparison between this system and the revised rules for dealing

with ancillary relief applications which were piloted in various courts and eventually extended nationwide in June 2000. One of the objections to the proposed new rules frequently expressed while they were being piloted was that particular local practices had been working well for many years and there was no need to fix a system which was not broken. These points of view did not prevail, the new rules which lay down a detailed procedure were introduced, and most observers now consider this to have brought about a considerable improvement.

The effect on other areas of legal practice

I have already mentioned the amendments to the rules governing ancillary relief applications. This process began, under the leadership of Mr Justice Thorpe, as he then was, in 1992 as an ad hoc group of family practitioners interested in reforming the procedure in ancillary relief cases. The group was subsequently adopted by the Lord Chancellor's Department and became the Lord Chancellor's Ancillary Relief Advisory Group and was finally renamed the President's Ancillary Relief Advisory Group (PARAG) in 2003. A new set of rules was devised and eventually approved by the Lord Chancellor and was piloted before being incorporated into the Family Proceedings Rules. The guiding principle is that the court directs the proceedings rather than allowing the parties to proceed at their own pace.

An important part of the new procedure is the Financial Dispute Resolution Appointment (FDR). This takes place when all evidence has been exchanged and the parties know what capital and other funds are available. The parties are required to attend before the district judge with their advocates and to disclose their without prejudice offers to settle. The function of the district judge is to define and narrow the issues and he does this by expressing a view on the merits or otherwise of the competing positions. This is definitely not a process of mediation or conciliation but it enables the parties and their lawyers to receive a preliminary indication of how the court is likely to deal with the case, and there is no doubt that it is a highly valuable and successful aid to settlement. Needless to say, the judge who conducts the FDR does not conduct the final hearing.

It would be going too far to say that the new system was directly based on the Bristol children scheme or any of the other schemes about the country. However, it must be remembered that the system which it replaced was extremely laissez faire and uncontrolled and that the frustration of practitioners must, to some extent, have arisen from seeing a more structured and rational system in operation in children's cases. Without that experience it is unlikely that the impetus for reform, and the institution of the FDR appointment, would have happened.

The Civil Procedure Rules

The final area of related developments to be considered is the civil procedure reforms of 1989 spearheaded by Lord Woolf (the Woolf reforms) which resulted in the new Civil Procedure Rules (CPR) which govern all non-family civil cases. The CPR provide for rigorous case management and court direction. Expert evidence is strictly controlled and hearings can never be vacated without the sanction of the court. Since the advent of the CPR in 2001, the face of civil litigation has changed out of all recognition.

Once again, it is difficult to show a strict causal link between the family reforms and the Woolf reforms. Nevertheless, there are striking similarities between the philosophy of case management and court control which resulted from the Children Act and the reforms of PARAG and what became the Woolf reforms. My personal view is that the Woolf reforms could never have happened without those earlier developments.

What of the future?

As I have suggested above, I think that the Family Proceedings Rules should be amended to contain much more prescriptive detail about the procedure which the courts should follow in children's cases. This procedure should apply to all courts and there should be no room for local variations.

A new scheme for children's cases is about to be piloted in London and it will be interesting to see what comes of this. It seems that a vital part of this procedure is to be the availability of an information/conciliation meeting before the issue of proceedings. This must be the correct way forward. All the evidence of the last 30 years is that the intervention of a mediator under the court's umbrella at a very early stage is vital for the resolution of the dispute.

In fact, I would go further and say that mediation at this early stage must become compulsory. Whether or not 'compulsory mediation' is an oxymoron is irrelevant (it is in reality what the court often imposes on the parties now). People who resort to the courts to resolve their disputes over children are usually in need of help, advice and support. Time and funds must be made available to provide that no application can reach a hearing until that help has been provided.

In that way, the aspirations of those who gathered at the university 25 years ago may finally be fulfilled.

Chapter 6

A RESEARCH PERSPECTIVE

Professor Gwynn Davis

Along with other contributors to this book I have a long, albeit intermittent association with family mediation. However, in my own case, being an academic researcher, the relationship has been that of investigator and commentator. What this means, psychologically and emotionally, is that I have never joined the family mediation 'movement', this being partly a matter of principle and partly, as kind friends have pointed out to me, a life position. This fits my conception of the researcher role, because research has a debunking tendency. If it is any good it will offer an alternative account to that advanced by practitioners and policy-makers. Accordingly, it suits iconoclastic personalities: the natural researcher is a borderline psychopath with just sufficient socialisation to avoid spending his entire life behind bars.

Personality aside, there are other features of the socio-legal research enterprise which it may be worth alluding to. First, research of this type does not take place in a vacuum: there are always other stories, and nowhere is this more apparent than in the sphere of law. A dominant theme of socio-legal research is the gap between the story advanced by law – 'law on the books' – and the way law works in practice: it is the gap between what *is* and what *is meant* to be. Secondly, socio-legal research typically gives prominence to the voice of the consumer of legal services: of course, everyone claims to speak for consumers, but other than through research the consumer's voice seldom emerges directly, except under conditions of ruthless editing. Thirdly, research will often focus upon the subterranean, that is to say, on low level and preliminary processes rather than on the major legal set-pieces, such as trials. Studies of family mediation fit perfectly within this tradition. And, finally, research is often concerned (too often, in my opinion) with monitoring innovation.[1]

None of this tells us whether the research in question is done well or badly, whether it is technically and intellectually rigorous or, perhaps, a triumph of presentation over content – a collection of brightly coloured charts and tables, culminating in portentous pronouncements. One might like to think that socio-legal research has a discerning readership, well able to sort the wheat from the chaff, but that is not obvious to me.

Researching the Bristol service

In 1979 I was green in judgement. Mervyn Murch had just given me my start in research, monitoring with him the ill-conceived 'Children's Appointments' which

---

[1] For those interested in this subject see 'Empirical Research in Law' by J Baldwin and G Davis in P Cane and M Tushnet, eds, *The Oxford Handbook of Legal Studies* (OUP, 2003).

comprised one element of the *Special Procedure* introduced in the mid-1970s as a means of streamlining undefended divorces.[1] We were based in Bristol University's Department of Social Administration (as it then was), under the leadership of the inspirational Roy Parker. The Bristol Courts Family Conciliation Service had just been launched, and it had applied to the Nuffield Foundation for a grant. Nuffield were keen to support this promising venture, but, in line with their standard practice when sponsoring innovation, they imposed a condition, namely that the service should be independently monitored (rather than that they should monitor themselves, as had been proposed). Nuffield would also fund the research. Accordingly, a researcher had to be found. A search was mounted and, probably through Mervyn's good offices, this callow youth was identified as potentially fitting the bill. I prepared a research proposal, which was accepted, and Mervyn released me from my contract with him for one day a week for 12 months so that I could carry out the work.

I have no recollection of how it was that I alighted upon the research methods employed in that early study. I did two things: first, I trawled through the service's early case records, doing my best on that limited evidence to arrive at some judgement of the mediator's contribution; and secondly, I interviewed 40 Bristol solicitors, all of them practising in the 'family' arena, a few of whom had actually referred clients to the Bristol service, asking them what they thought of conciliation. Needless to say, some had barely considered this subject and most had no actual experience to go on, but, faced with my anxious promptings, they did their best to offer an opinion.

I see now, as I did not see then, that these were not powerful research methods. The gap between the research questions posed and the intended means of answering them was painfully wide. The report that I produced was predictably anodyne, although it was broadly supportive of the work of the service since such evidence as I had collected did indeed point in that direction.

This did not save me from criticism from within BCFCS, it being observed that I had failed to represent the views of the mediators. This alleged deficiency troubled Lisa Parkinson in particular, and at that stage I was ill-equipped to respond, as I should do today, by enquiring how it would have benefited anyone for me to have added a third, even less penetrating research method to the two that I had already employed. I was required to attend a meeting of the service's Management Committee in order to explain myself. My (possibly over-heated) recollection is that I was brought to that meeting in handcuffs. I was certainly in the doghouse, and required to account for my deficiencies. It was one of those 'small ... scorching ordeals which fire one's irresolute clay'.[2] A summary of my research report was later published as an Appendix to the Legal Aid Annual Reports.[3]

---

[1]   That research was funded by the Joseph Rowntree Memorial Trust.
[2]   C Day Lewis: 'Walking Away'.
[3]   'Report of a research to monitor the work of the Bristol Courts Family Conciliation Service in its first year of operation', 30th Legal Aid Annual Reports (1979–80), Appendix D, (Lord Chancellor's Department, 1981).

Continuing debates

My direct engagement with family mediation practice ceased for a time after this early foray, although I continued to take an interest in – and occasionally contributed to – ongoing debates concerning its precise character, distinguishing features, and relationship to legal processes. Some of these debates have continued for 25 years, and it is one of the more remarkable features of family mediation as a practice innovation that it has been so fiercely fought over, both within and beyond its ranks. Amongst the issues debated are:

– whether mediation is necessarily separate from legal processes (with the inevitable imposition of external authority) or whether there is a continuum from independent, non-coercive third-party assisted negotiation through to court-inspired 'mediation' as a fillip to pre-trial negotiation (or horse-trading);
– whether mediation is distinguished by its emphasis on party control, or whether its practice is compatible with the application of expressly therapeutic interventions with their arcane theoretical rationales; and
– whether, even if mediation is *about children* (which it generally was, in the early days), it is essentially a matter of adult-to-adult negotiation with, again, party-control as its centrepiece, or whether the mediator is entitled to present herself as a child welfare expert and seek to impose her vision of the child's best interests upon one, or conceivably both parents.[1]

I once believed that there were right and wrong answers to these questions, but on the whole I think the researcher's task is to scrutinise the various accounts of what is going on and to point out the extent to which practice does or does not conform to the language employed. Rather than be too concerned about preserving the 'purity' or separateness of mediation, the researcher is better employed in trying to help everyone, including the customers of these various services, understand what it is they offer. The same applies to the service provided by lawyers and courts. I do not think researchers should be prescriptive, but they should provide accurate descriptions – and, where something is being misdescribed, offer an alternative account.

The one exception I made to this concerned an attempt by some therapeutically inclined members of the family court welfare service (now, of course, CAFCASS) to apply the language of conciliation to forms of intervention which rested on abstruse theoretical constructs which were never explained to the parents involved, and certainly would not have been understood by them. The abuse of language in some of these accounts was troubling, and the abuse of power even more so. Lionel Trilling put it better than I could:

'Some paradox of our nature leads us, when once we have made our fellow man the object of our enlightened interest, to go on to make them the objects of our pity, then our wisdom, ultimately our coercion.'[2]

---

[1]   There is also, these days, debate concerning whether children should be involved directly.
[2]   L Trilling, *The Liberal Imagination* (1953), at p 214, quoted by Robert J Levy in (1984) *Family Law Quarterly*, at p 533.

Mediation and legal proceedings

Just as the Bristol service was pioneering the development of family mediation, an inventive registrar at Bristol County Court, Geoffrey Parmiter, was identifying the potential for the court itself, through its judicial officers and the family court welfare service, to sponsor legal settlement in a way never before attempted, with the registrar and welfare officer occupying quasi-mediating roles.[1] Parmiter was not greatly interested in mediation as an alternative to court proceedings; he was an administrator who found himself frustrated by the delays and inefficiencies of the litigation process, and who, well before these notions gained general acceptance, hit on the twin ideas of court-sponsored settlement and court control of the litigation timetable. Geoffrey was not trying to promote party control and, had the idea been put to him, it is unlikely he would have been sympathetic: he probably did not think that these people should have been cluttering up his court in the first place.

The fact that mediation (or 'conciliation' as it was still referred to) should have appealed to an administrator manqué like Geoffrey Parmiter and to those (like Simon Roberts) who saw the potential for removing most divorce disputes from lawyers altogether, not to mention its attraction to family therapists, gives some indication of the bewildering multiplicity of values, attitudes and approaches to which this term was being applied. Marc Galanter collapsed these various strands into two when he suggested that enthusiasm for mediation was based on either a 'warm' theme or a 'cool' theme. The warm theme referred to the aspiration to bring the parties to a mutual accord; the cool theme was concerned with efficient institutional management, reducing cost and delay, and unburdening the court.

The public face of family mediation, and the generally laudatory reception that it received in the media, emphasised the warm theme. But family mediation services, with BCFCS in the vanguard, sought public funding, and government was interested only in the cool theme. This meant that the Bristol service, and others, felt bound to assert that mediation had the potential to pay for itself – better still, to save public money – by reducing demand on both the legal aid fund and the courts. They not only felt bound to assert it; they probably believed it.

I think it fair to say that I realised, without having undertaken any research on the subject, that this claim was likely to be mistaken. The same conclusion could, I believe, have been reached by any first-year sociology student.[2] It seemed obvious to me that government expenditure on family lawyers – which those practitioners, not unreasonably, deemed to be inadequate – could only be controlled at source. Whatever success family mediators had in individual cases would do little to reduce demand on legal aid – a demand which at that time appeared to be rising inexorably. What is more, the argument that mediators were much cheaper than lawyers was based on a form of false accounting under which mediation appeared to be cheap because it was performed by volunteers, or by family court welfare

---

[1]   GM Parmiter, 'Bristol In-Court Conciliation Procedure' (1981) *Law Society Gazette*, 78.
[2]   Since this happens to be the full extent of my formal education in sociology, I am naturally inclined to regard it as sufficient.

officers whose true costs were absorbed by the probation service. If mediators were paid out of public funds, as they aspired to be, they could prove quite expensive. I made these points on various occasions, including in a book called *Partisans and Mediators* which I worked on through much of the 1980s:

> 'Apart from the innate implausibility of the savings argument, those who make such claims tend to forget that the legal profession has grown, if not fat, then at least numerous on the strength of legal aid. Whenever steps are taken to reduce this expenditure, for example in simplifying procedure, or in transferring work to a lower court, one observes the legal profession negotiating a higher hourly rate, or increasing the number of applications made in respect of other matters, or simply managing, within each case, to locate more chargeable work. Short of some natural catastrophe which decimates the number of fee-earning matrimonial lawyers, the demands on the legal aid fund will continue to rise. Mediation cannot change this.'[1]

In due course, at the instigation of a reforming Lord Chancellor,[2] this 'natural catastrophe' did indeed come to pass, but it had nothing to do with mediation.

I had in the meantime (this was in the mid-1980s) been awarded a further grant by the Nuffield Foundation to study 'in court' conciliation procedures of the type instigated by Geoffrey Parmiter in Bristol. This was the first time that I had attempted a large scale 'consumer' study of legal proceedings, and the results were disconcerting. The key finding was that many parents experienced an almost complete loss of authority and loss of control during these court-based negotiations – far removed, in other words, from Galanter's warm theme. Many cases were subject to repeated adjournments and repeated 'mediations', with the eventual settlement arrived at through a process of attrition. The bargain, or compromise, reigned supreme. What is more, issues of authority were blurred to such an extent that some parents could not distinguish between the 'mediation' which they had experienced and a full-blown trial. Some thought there had indeed been a trial: their case had been 'settled', but they thought it had been adjudicated.

At some point in the future, when researchers rule the world, findings such as these will have an immediate and dramatic impact on policy. We are not there yet, however, and no-one seemed too concerned that the language of mediation was being applied to highly coercive procedures. As far as courts were concerned, settlement was the thing. And why was this? Well, there were two reasons, and they still apply today. First, when it comes to disputes about children, the judiciary have no confidence in their own product. Judges themselves believe that courts are a blunt instrument which cannot hope to grapple with the complexity and rival versions of truth which characterise issues of residence or contact – they think there must be a better way. And secondly, there is rationing. This I think is the main reason; the rationing motif dominates our system of private family law. The principal objective is not to supply a service; it is instead to restrict access to a service, the service in question being judicial determination. Courts have no wish to make themselves *more* accessible to warring parents, or to explore the issues

---

dividing them in any depth; they want them out of the door, preferably never to return. There is little interest in the value of settlements arrived at in these circumstances: they may make no contribution to a resolution of the problem as it is experienced by the parties, but no-one will know this.

This is why the distinction between settlement and resolution, which I first heard enunciated by Roy Parker in a lecture to an invited audience at Bristol University in 1980, is of fundamental importance. This is the distinction between, on the one hand, putting a stop to overt conflict and on the other, achieving genuine agreement, or harmony. This distinction is central to an understanding of the merits and limitations of all conflict-resolving strategies, and yet it is seldom referred to, other than perhaps by implication.[1]

The Inter-departmental Committee

It was one of the jokes of the *Yes Minister* television programme that in time of difficulty, and particularly when under pressure to act, the Minister would set up an Inter-departmental Committee. In 1982 the Lord Chancellor, Lord Hailsham, found himself under pressure from the family conciliation lobby, and the Inter-departmental Committee was duly appointed. The world-weary cynicism of this manoeuvre was reflected in the Committee's brief, which was 'to review current arrangements for conciliation … within existing resource planning'. The Committee was chaired by a Mr Robinson, who was an official in the Lord Chancellor's Department (LCD). Mr Robinson's fame had not spread beyond Whitehall, and the embryonic conciliation services, all of whom would have sacrificed their grandmothers for a hint of government funding, viewed his appointment with fear and nervous anticipation. In fact, those of us interested in the subject at the time had become used to a succession of officials (several of them named Robinson) who emerged before our wondering eyes at some conference or other to announce that, henceforward, they were responsible for the Department's policy in this area. Observing the pinstriped suit and the confident demeanour, the delegates wondered what, if anything, this person knew about the subject, and whether he was indeed the saviour they were looking for: could it possibly be that beneath this not very appealing exterior there lurked qualities of wisdom and judgement sufficient to shepherd this bawling infant into the tender embrace of government?

This particular Mr Robinson was certainly no saviour. His Committee reported in July 1983, having asked itself whether a national conciliation service funded by government would be likely to pay for itself through savings in court time and legal aid. The problem, as I have made plain, lay not in the Robinson Committee's answer to this question (which was in the negative), but in the question itself, which was not so much a question as a breathtakingly self-confident assertion of the superordinate status of lawyers, courts and all things legal. Sometimes, when I hear Stephen Cretney complain that the Lord Chancellor's Department (or the Department for Constitutional Affairs, as it now is) no longer finds it necessary to appoint lawyers to its staff, preferring to recruit from amongst those with degrees

---

[1]   See G Davis, 'Conciliation and the Professions' (1983) *Family Law* 6, at 13.

in marketing or golf club management – and even as I might be tempted to agree with him – I wonder if he remembers the various Mr Robinsons. For they were doubtless all lawyers, and it was those lawyers who, on being put in charge of an area of social policy, could not ask themselves a single sensible question. They could only act as representatives of the professional legal interest. Admittedly, this may not have been entirely their fault – civil servants do the bidding of their political masters – but as an expression of government thinking at that time, the Robinson report was a dispiriting document.

The Newcastle research

The government probably hoped that the Robinson report would see the back of all these importunate mediators, but the pressures continued, prompting the LCD to resort to another well-known diversionary tactic, that of the blockbuster research exercise. At the time I argued strongly against giving all this money to one centre, and also against the grandiose research brief. Government departments with no in-house research expertise should not ask detailed research questions, let alone impose a complex methodology involving surveys, control groups, and the like. As it was, the Newcastle team accepted what I had thought was the discredited conflation of 'in-court' and 'out-of-court' mediation as forming a single research subject, and set about comparing the cost-effectiveness of the one with the other. The researchers established to their satisfaction that mediation on court premises was more cost-effective than the out-of-court variety. They also proposed 'a new model for a national conciliation service in which conciliation would be one part of a network of local services, independent of the courts and the probation service, to be called The Family Advisory, Counselling and Conciliation Bureau'.

This 'vision' had already been rejected by the Robinson Committee and so was unlikely to be implemented, but elements of it have re-emerged from time to time in the course of other research undertaken by the Newcastle team, most notably in their monitoring of the abortive Information Meetings introduced as part of the Family Law Act 1996 and, more recently, in their work on the Legal Services Commission's 'Family Advice and Information Networks'.

Hybridity

The case for some element of government funding for mediation continued to be argued, despite this second dose of cold water, with many family lawyers also committing themselves to the cause. Indeed, it was becoming difficult to separate mediation from solicitors' own practice. There was developing in some centres a complex inter-relationship between supposedly independent mediation services and the courts, with couples passing back and forth between the two. Meanwhile, customers of mediation services might find that their mediator was in fact a lawyer, engaged in mediation as a kind of secondary activity. Even if the mediator's antecedents were impeccably 'social', he or she was likely to be a good deal preoccupied with achieving agreements that could be presented to a court as constituting a legal settlement. So, increasingly, we had mediation in the law, and we had law in mediation. We had deflection from the formal, and formalisation of the informal.

An important component of this hybridity was a gradual evolution in the practice of family lawyers, with mediation a significant influence. Solicitors specialising in family law had long prided themselves on their distinctive approach to litigation: whilst undeniably partisan, they also professed a responsibility towards the family as a whole, particularly the children. Accordingly, they did not aim to 'win' their cases; their role, as they saw it, was to accompany and guide the client through the process. In their dealings with 'the other side' they exercised restraint – or at least, claimed to. In most centres they comprised a small, clubbable, friendly group. They also prided themselves on their ability to deflect their clients from their more self-mutilating strategies. They renounced trials. They were no longer, except in extremis, advocates. The emphasis had long switched to negotiation, and their approach to that negotiation reflected a complex mix of: (a) the lawyer's perception of both the individual client's and the broader family interest; (b) the normative standards set by the legal framework; and (c) the client's own input.[1]

Little of this was reflected in public debate concerning the future of family mediation, and nor was it understood within government. Officials in the Lord Chancellor's Department had, by and large, been persuaded that they should throw their weight behind mediation as the preferred alternative to 'litigation'. The approach of family lawyers tended, therefore, to be caricatured. So, for example, in the Access to Justice Act 1999, concerned with the reform of legal aid, it was asserted (s 8) that in many family disputes 'mediation will be more appropriate than court proceedings'.

The Family Law Act 1996

Despite mediation's favourable press, and despite what appeared to be an increasingly receptive policy environment, family mediators were not over-whelmed with demand for their services. This drove them into an uncomfortable alliance[2] with that strand of government thinking which is characterised by an unswerving confidence in its own judgement on social issues, and a determination to foist the results of that judgement on its citizens in order to do them good. We now think of this as a characteristic of New Labour, but it was also manifested in the Family Law Act 1996, a curiously pre-Blairite measure with its array of guiding, deflecting, information-providing measures, such 'information' to be, of course, neutral and uncontested.

None of this could reasonably be expected to trouble family mediators since, clearly, the central plank of 'information' envisaged by the Act was the information that mediation was a jolly good thing. What is more, Part III of the Act committed public money to the support of mediation services and, as a means of stimulating 'demand', required prospective legal aid applicants to explore the mediation option. Section 29 of the Act stipulated that, before securing legal aid for lawyer representation, the applicant would need to attend a meeting with a

---

[1]   There are many accounts of this practice. See, for example, G Davis, S Cretney and J Collins, *Simple Quarrels* (Clarendon Press, 1992); or J Eekelaar, M Maclean and S Beinart, *Family Lawyers: The Divorce Work of Solicitors* (Hart Publishing, 2000).

[2]   Although I am not sure how much discomfort was actually felt; probably not much.

mediator.[1] Section 29 would, it was hoped, deliver a substantial tranche of new customers to mediation. (They would all be at the lower end of the market, financially speaking, since the requirement applied only to those seeking legal aid, which is of course means-tested; the rich remained free to litigate to their heart's content.)

Unusually, this aspect of the legislation was monitored prior to full implementation,[2] and I led the research team which undertook the task. Since our customer was the Legal Aid Board (now the Legal Services Commission (LSC)), it was inevitable that we would give considerable attention to the question of whether, under the institutional arrangements then in place, mediation was likely to prove cost-effective. This was not discriminatory. The same rigour, and relative parsimony, was by this stage being applied to lawyer funding under the LSC's new regime of contracting with individual suppliers. The days of legal aid as a demand-led service were over. It was bad luck on the mediation 'industry' that it should achieve public funding at the very point when the whole of civil legal aid became subject to contracting (in other words, at the point when payment became tied to case throughput, and even, as far as mediation was concerned, to outcome). This had all become necessary because civil legal aid had seen explosive increases in expenditure through the late 1980s and early 1990s. Paying private practitioners by the hour out of public funds had proved massively inflationary. So family mediation secured public funding, but subject to this new contracting regime.

The research team set itself to answer the question of which services, or combination of services, would deliver reasonable outcomes for a substantial element of the separating population at reasonable cost. Cost had, of course, to be linked to 'benefits' – however one defined benefits. The systems of onward referral and assessment introduced under Part III of the Family Law Act 1996 had considerable influence upon the outcome of the various comparisons being attempted. We were monitoring one specific mechanism for supporting mediation out of public funds, and a rather peculiar gatekeeping device.

This mechanism undermined the cost-effectiveness of mediation overall. It was spectacularly inefficient, the main problem being that it is a fundamentally different matter to determine legal aid eligibility on an individual basis than it is to determine eligibility for mediation, which requires the participation of both parties. The non-legally-aided person can undermine mediation in a way that he or she cannot undermine participation in legal proceedings because the latter are unashamedly coercive. This basic weakness rendered s 29 largely ineffective, requiring mediation services to devote much of their resources to preliminary assessments that had little prospect of transforming the chrysalis of 'intake' into the iridescent butterfly of mediation.

We were also trying to gain some measure of value. For reasons already explained, 'settlement' could not be the only yardstick, since almost anything delivers settlement, including, most obviously, delay. The other benefits of mediation are

---

[1]   There were exceptions under which this obligation could be waived.
[2]   As were the Information Meetings, by a team from Newcastle University.

often asserted, but are not easily researchable. The best one can do, generally speaking, is ask the parties whether they had found the process beneficial. On these soft measures of customer satisfaction, mediation achieves more than adequate approval ratings. For example, in our survey, 35 per cent of those of who had experienced mediation in respect of a dispute about children had found it 'very helpful', and a further 51 per cent had found it 'fairly helpful'. Seventy-one per cent said they would recommend mediation to others who were experiencing similar difficulties.

It was noteworthy, however, that on all the soft measures of approval that we employed, solicitors achieved significantly higher ratings. For example, in relation to disputes about children, 60 per cent (compared to 35 per cent) had found their solicitor 'very helpful'. It is important here to acknowledge that we were not comparing like with like. Solicitors are partisan advisers and supporters, whereas mediators are non-aligned. (Had we asked our informants for their view of *their spouse's* solicitor, we would no doubt have gained an altogether different view of the legal profession, as being comprised of crooks and sadists.) But the high approval ratings that our informants granted their own solicitor should not be dismissed. They indicate that the service provided to these people by their lawyers is highly valued, and that it meets their needs.

Lawyers and mediators

The implications of this research evidence for the future of family mediation are not easily determined, but my take on these matters is as follows. First, we need to be clear about what it is that lawyers offer. Lawyers provide partisan support, coupled with an authoritative account of the norms of legal settlement. Both of these are valued. The lawyer's remit is, therefore, broader than that of the mediator. For the separating couple, the legal adviser connotes authority, and through that authority, a measure of psychological containment. In so far as mediators provide this, they do so by investing the performance of their role with features that are not intrinsic to it and do not figure in any ideal type characterisation.

One should not, therefore, aim to replace lawyers with mediators. It is unfortunate, in my view, that the policy debate has focused on diversion – on mediators' capacity to deliver what lawyers deliver, but at reduced cost. The demand for lawyers will always be strong, and can only be controlled through rationing. In order to have an impact on the volume of legal activity, and the cost of that activity, these matters have to be tackled directly. If this is the test which mediation is required to pass, it is being set up to fail.

Mediation should be viewed as a separate, parallel service which can make an important contribution by helping to resolve a significant minority of separation-based disputes. Its practitioners must try to resist judgement by measures of value which are wholly legal-centric, such as diversion from legal proceedings, or conclusion of those proceedings without resort to trial. Mediators should identify independent measures of value, and insist upon them. These will inevitably be 'soft' – for example, improved communication and understanding. But these soft measures matter to the parties, and they may well be more meaningful than the achievement of a court order, which is often of no use to anyone. Mediation symbolises an alternative version of empowerment to that represented by lawyers and courts – one that rests on participation and engagement. This may be a minority choice under the stresses of relationship breakdown, but it is nonetheless important to offer it.

There remains, in addition, the possibility of employing mediation as a court-based settlement strategy. Mediation in this context will take on many of the other features of late-stage litigation; that is to say, it will be characterised by bargaining and pressure, including cost pressure, and by the imposition of third party judgement. It will not in general be informed by the values which underpin mediation when it is practised independently of legal proceedings.

There remain difficult questions concerning how best to bring mediation to the attention of those who might benefit from it. One can understand mediators' frustration (and scepticism) at having to rely on solicitors for their cases. That is like relying on GPs to refer patients to a branch of alternative medicine. But diverting couples to mediation as a kind of gatekeeping device within legal aid is never going to work satisfactorily, in my view, because it is too prescriptive. We should encourage separating couples to opt for mediation at whatever point makes sense to them. This could be adjacent to legal proceedings, but it could also be much earlier, or much later. I therefore believe we should give up on gatekeeping devices which divert people from lawyers to mediators without their necessarily understanding what is going on. The emphasis within the Family Law Act 1996 upon *process*, and upon choosing one process over another at a time when people are facing a crisis in their lives, requires them to focus upon questions which they do not feel equipped to answer and whose import they do not understand. We should also be cautious, in general, about restricting access to a service which people feel they need, or in pressing them to consume a service which they have not recognised they need. Family mediation should not have to rely on that. It may be a minority choice, but it is not a small minority, and satisfied customers will continue to speak for it.

Chapter 7

EXPANSION OF LOCAL SERVICES INTO A NATIONAL NETWORK AND THE SETTING OF NATIONAL STANDARDS

Thelma Fisher

Family mediation in the UK began in the 1970s at a time of rapid social change, often termed 'post-modernity', which profoundly affected marriage and family patterns. Society had to adjust and mediation has been part of that adjustment. Noel Timms in the Newcastle University Conciliation Unit (CPU) Project report in 1989,[1] wrote of mediators introducing a 'new social practice' and Gwynn Davis wrote frequently of the pressure on mediators to prove their effectiveness alongside the long-established legal profession. Mediators were creating a new discipline to assist families caught up in the changes occurring on such a large scale that they were exceeding the remits of 'justice' and 'welfare' carried out by courts and public social services. This chapter takes up the story of the expansion of family mediation into a national network of providers and a national system for setting and regulating standards of practice.

First phase of national development: a network of local services and an evolving practice (1981–1988)

Local committees

Family mediation development first took place in local family conciliation services managed by committees of professional people and community representatives. These recruited and arranged the training of the conciliators whom they then supervised and managed. As has been described, the Bristol Service was the first in the line. Practically every new service was drawn into a national network initiated by Bristol and a few early services; this was called the National Family Conciliation Council (NFCC), operating through a democratic committee structure linked to local committees. Services met annually at AGMs which came to define the landmarks of the story. This pattern laid the foundations of what later became National Family Mediation (NFM) and was characteristic of the way not-for-profit (then called 'voluntary sector') bodies formed and behaved in the 1970s in order to test and grow a new idea.

---

[1] Lord Chancellor's Department, 'Report on the Costs and Effectiveness of Conciliation in England and Wales' (University of Newcastle, 1989).

A national network

I entered the story in 1981 as the first employee when Swindon mimicked its big sister in Bristol by creating a local service. I attended the first national gathering in Birmingham, described by Lisa Parkinson in her chapter, and was a member of the steering committee that devised the organisational structure of the NFCC and made an early attempt at national standards – first on the back of an envelope in a pub in Chancery Lane. We proceeded to vet services' committee structures and mediator qualifications before admitting them as provisional and then full members. Help was offered with training as well as with development. On approving the first Code of Practice,[1] NFCC made adherence to it a requirement of membership. A quarterly newsletter was inaugurated and a retired Court Welfare Officer, Jack Chapman, both wrote it and, when we succeeded in getting any national media coverage, responded by hand to every enquiry from the public. (On giving up this task, he handed on to me pages of stamps of different values, dating from years back, to use as an economy measure.)

National promotion

By the time the number of services had reached 45, the national committee, always with a Bristol member, was collecting and analysing national statistics and taking collective action to draw attention to the funding crises of member services by drawing in Members of Parliament and recruiting a parliamentary spokesman. From the inauguration of the Bristol Service, the redoubtable Baroness Faithfull championed mediation in the House of Lords and elsewhere because of her deep concern about children. We also interested well-known journalists such as Claire Rayner and Katherine Whitehorn. NFCC's public focus was unhesitatingly children. This was fuelled by the first UK research studies which picked up the baton passed from the USA by Judith Wallerstein and Joan Kelly.[2] Yvette Walczak and Sheila Burns in London collected stories from young adults whose parents had divorced[3] and Ann Mitchell[4] walked the streets of Edinburgh tracking down and interviewing children whose parents had divorced in a particular year. A long-term cohort study[5] showed mostly negative effects of divorce on children. These studies created a platform for promoting the benefits of mediation in reducing conflict and long-term damage to children.

Co-operation within the Family Justice System

At local level, mediation had to be fitted into what else was available in the area. Most committees followed Bristol's constitution and consisted of representatives from the local Marriage Guidance Council (now Relate), the newly specialising family court welfare officers, the Citizens Advice Bureau and local solicitors – in fact the very people into whose practices mediators had to dovetail their own. Thus

---

[1]　In L Parkinson, *Conciliation in Separation and Divorce* (Croomhelm, 1986).

[2]　JS Wallerstein and JB Kelly, *Surviving the Breakup: How Children and Parents Cope with Divorce* (New York: Basic Books, 1980).

[3]　Y Walczak and S Burns *Divorce; The Child's Point of View* (Harper and Row, 1984).

[4]　A Mitchell, *Children in the Middle: Living through Divorce* (Tavistock Publications, 1985).

[5]　M Maclean and MEJ Wadsworth 'The interests of children after parental divorce: A long-term perspective' (1988) *International Journal of Law and the Family*, 2, 155–166.

co-operation to improve local provision for this growing group of families was twinned to carefulness not to displace what already existed. At national level, the same blend of co-operation and avoidance of competition operated while the legal establishment adjusted to two new voices in its midst – the Solicitors Family Law Association (SFLA) and NFCC. Prompted by the proposals of the Finer Report recommending a family court, the Family Court Campaign was a great unifying cause, which in its time, proposed and costed how all could work together within a family court framework; NFCC like others proposed mediation structures. After a visit from the Association of Family and Conciliation Courts from the USA, for whom we organised a conference at the LSE, the UK formed the Standing Conference for Interdisciplinary Co-operation in Family Proceedings (nicknamed 'Skidcops') which brought professional groups together over a number of years to share their experience and understanding. This was hugely influential in co-ordinating the professional response to the new concept of parental responsibility in the Children Act 1989.

Early practice and standards

Although the basic requirements of the mediator role and mediation's professional ethics were set out in the early literature and the Code of Practice,[1] how exactly the process itself could best be made to work took longer to discover. An American book written by JM Haynes, found its way to the UK[2] while we were coming to terms, by trial and error, with using a new process and with the impact of close encounters with other people's separating marriages – their anguish and their children's helplessness in the face of it. Different ways of conducting mediation were beginning to emerge and be shared. Sometimes a model seems to have evolved from the way a service was set up; for example, if it was founded by linking an out-of-hours court welfare officer with a marriage counsellor, mediation would be conducted by two mediators with[3] or without a defined theoretical underpinning; or a service might adopt a therapeutic approach as a result of the introduction of family systems theory[4] into the training of the court welfare officers instrumental in setting up the mediation service. Sometimes, the mediators and supervisor worked out their own ways. In Swindon, a committee member tracked recorded instances of domestic violence from mediation case notes which led to a return to separate first appointments, which, in some other services, were either de rigueur or strenuously avoided, but for quite different reasons. A joint workshop with ACAS mediators working in collective conciliation clarified the common procedural stages of mediation, regardless of model. In visits to the UK, John Haynes demonstrated his blend of mediation strategies and techniques adapted from industrial mediation and family therapy questionning techniques. These influences, backed by the earlier general account of disputes and negotiations by Gulliver,[5] mark the start of the delineation of the skills now enshrined in the UK College of Family Mediators ('The College') standard for assessing individual mediator competence. Children issues were the sole focus of family mediation until

---

[1]   In L Parkinson, *Conciliation in Separation and Divorce* (Croomhelm, 1986).

[2]   JM Haynes, *Divorce Mediation* (Springer, 1981).

[3]   J Coogler, *Structured Mediation in Divorce Settlements* (Lexington, 1978).

[4]   J Howard and G Shepherd, *Conciliation, Children and Divorce* (Batsford, 1987).

[5]   PH Gulliver, *Disputes and Negotiations: A Cross-cultural Perspective* (Academic Press, 1979).

1988 when what was to become the Family Mediators Association (FMA) developed a model of mediation in the private sector which brought together a family mediator and a lawyer mediator to help couples resolve all the issues of their divorce.

Second phase of development: the sophistication of practice and the politicisation of mediation (1989–1995)

The Children Act 1989 marks the next phase of the story. A harbinger of change, it surely affected the readiness of trustees of major Trusts to back the development of mediation. The Nuffield Foundation and Children in Need awarded grants to NFCC to set up a serious national body with paid central staff. The three objectives were to develop an effective national structure, a framework for national practice standards and the promotion of mediation to the divorcing public. During this period the number of local services increased to 68, Professor Brenda Hale (now The Rt Hon Baroness Hale of Richmond) was appointed as the first outside chair, adding her clear voice and creative influence, and a new honorary treasurer, Richard Tickell, improved fund-raising.

National selection, training and accreditation

Following a grant by the Joseph Rowntree Foundation, a national training programme was devised which was tested and modified by a selected team of trainers and then delivered stage by stage to every mediator in the NFCC network. This brought mediators together nationally and regionally and began to standardise good practice. This was followed by the introduction of an accreditation procedure carried out by local supervisors and national assessors which used the same list of skills identified in training. An innovatory national selection procedure was introduced which included the identification of aptitude for mediation.

All Issues Mediation

The second landmark of the period was the publication in April 1989 of the government commissioned Newcastle University's CPU report on conciliation.[1] Although equivocal on cost, it highlighted the good practice of many mediators and the positive response of many couples to mediation thus encouraging further development. The finding that many of the resolutions of disputes about children were undermined by continuing disputes about money was the basis of an NFCC application to the Joseph Rowntree Foundation for a grant to develop comprehensive mediation in the not-for-profit sector. Could the not-for-profit sector also provide this option for its consumers and, if so, how might this be made to work within the structure of a local service? A 2-year project, linked to a further Newcastle University research programme, tracked the development[2] of five local services, one of them inevitably Bristol, as they tried different models whereby family lawyers and, in one case a welfare rights specialist, joined the mediator at

---

[1] Lord Chancellor's Department *Report on the Costs and Effectiveness of Conciliation in England and Wales* (University of Newcastle, 1989).

[2] J Walker, P McCarthy, and N Timms, *Mediation: the Making and Remaking of Co-operative Relationships: An evaluation of the effectiveness of comprehensive mediation* (NCFS, 1994).

certain stages of the process. The research report showed greater levels of client satisfaction when all issues were resolved and showed that there was little difference in the results in relation to the models used. A training course was devised and work begun in providing it to local services.

Children in mediation

There were by now diametrically opposed voices about the role of children in mediation, some seeing mediation as an entirely adult business and others wanting to explore how children might be appropriately involved so that plans for them took their views and feelings into account. Bristol, like many others, 'saw' children occasionally. A grant was sought to develop this area of practice and services were actively consulted about their views. Common ground was found in the concept of consultation – indirectly (parents consulting children themselves) or directly (mediators consulting children and bringing their views back to parents). A final report on the study was written[1] from which a training course was developed.

Domestic violence

Early in 1989, researchers asked NFCC if they could study how mediators tackled domestic violence. The attitudes and practices of mediators were therefore studied at a time when awareness of domestic violence among all professionals was low. Awareness was raised by the exercise among both family court welfare officers and family mediators. The report was followed by the development of a training course for mediators in screening for domestic violence jointly developed with the help of the research team.[2]

Politicisation of mediation

In 1993, Lord Mackay, the Lord Chancellor published a Consultation (Green) Paper on the reform of divorce, which included a summary of the scheme recommended by the Law Commission in 1990,[3] and used the term 'mediation' in its title.[4] NFCC had just moved from Swindon to a small London office and the Green Paper's title took the media by surprise which all but overwhelmed the new office in faxes and telephone requests for interviews. For the next 2 years leading up to the publication of the Family Law Bill in 1995, mediator organisations worked to meet the challenge for which they had campaigned – the appropriate integration of mediation into the family justice system. Lord Mackay even talked of a presumption in favour of mediation rather than litigation.[5] NFCC adopted the term 'mediation', though not without some regional protests, eventually becoming

---

[1] National Family Mediation, 'Giving Children a Voice in Mediation: a study of mediation practice carried out by National Family Mediation with the help of the Calouste Gulbenkian Foundation (1994).

[2] M Hester, C Pearson, and L Radford 'Domestic Violence: A national survey of court welfare and voluntary sector mediation practice' (1997).

[3] HMSO Law Com No 192, 'Family Law: The ground for divorce' (1990).

[4] The Lord Chancellor's Department 'Looking to the future: Mediation and the ground for divorce', a consultation paper (1993).

[5] National Family Mediation Address by the Lord Chancellor to the Annual General Meeting 7 December 1994.

National Family Mediation (NFM). A new inter-professional group called The Mediation Forum (evolved from an advisory body to FMA) was chaired by the Director of the National Council for Family Proceedings (NCFP previously 'Skidcops'). It turned its attention to the provision of information to those divorcing, one of the proposals in Law Com 192. In unconscious anticipation of later pilots providing information, this group, chaired by a Director of the Nuffield Foundation, actually costed and presented a scheme to the government, that would be run by an inter-professional committee in each region. As in the case of the Children Act, when the Family Law Bill was presented to Parliament, there was a flurry of inter-professional activity which eventually settled into lobbying meetings to which mediators contributed – one co-ordinated by the Law Society, another by the marriage organisations and a third by the Children's Charities. En route, NFM set up a Mediation Exhibition in the House of Commons in which SFLA and FMA took part and regularly attended the Parliamentary Group for Children chaired by Baroness Faithfull. There were conferences at St George's, Windsor and at Leeds Castle in which politicians also took part.

The UK College of Family Mediators (The College)

In January 1994, a Symposium took place at Regent's College between NFM and FMA members attended also by Family Mediation Scotland. A small group, again including Kay Begg from Bristol, had been working to prepare for such an event and the large number of participants who attended voted to pursue the formation of a single professional body for family mediators. Work was carried out to bring this into being in readiness for the progress of the Bill through Parliament. Although this book has focused on experience south of the border, the search for parity of standards has always included Scotland and Northern Ireland.

The passage of the Family Law Bill

There was little doubt that the most important task for the national bodies was the briefing of members of all parties in both Houses of Parliament during the passage of the Family Law Bill. This became less a matter of promoting mediation than distinguishing repeatedly what it was from what it was not. The word 'mediation' was continually in danger of being used to support whatever members were moved to say about marriage and divorce. One fascination of the debates lay in the under-currents which swelled to become its driving forces. These were twofold: generational differences which polarised into an older generation trying to turn the clock back and a younger generation willing to legislate for the changes taking place. These were only marginally about political affiliation and 'mediation', usually misunderstood, would be variously seen as either a way of stopping change or of promoting it; the second force was the often extreme behaviour generated by the imminent collapse of the Conservative government and the parts played in that drama by the Labour front bench and the Conservative back bench. The Family Law Act 1996 was passed, but its original simplicity was destroyed.

Third phase: Government-funded development of national provision of family mediation(1996–2000)

The effects of the Family Law Act on family mediators

I often seek reassurance from mediators that they do not regret the work done in the 1990s to fund their work. I can look back with nostalgia to the early days of pioneering this 'new social practice' without the bureaucracy that now accompanies it. Along with the £3 million[1] eventual investment by the government to set up locally franchised, quality assured, national family mediation provision came the development of assessed competence, tight financial management of the receipt and spending of public money and initially clumsy procedures for getting legally aided clients into the mediation room. The strain of pressured demands on voluntary management committees and treasurers was great. Many mediators felt that their efforts to preserve the flexibility of sensitive practice were seen as blocks to progress in the eyes of a rapidly re-organising Legal Services Commission (LSC). To this were added the constraints and anxieties of another large-scale research study, this one making comparisons of consumer value and cost effectiveness between an established and effective family solicitor service to individuals and a rapidly developing mediation service for couples where the outcomes of new and experienced mediators were uniformly measured suggesting that experience counted for little. The report[2] included a very interesting profile of the mediation client population and found that mediators were highly appreciated by clients (as were family solicitors) but again mediation cost findings were equivocal partly because multi-variate analysis was used and partly because insufficient cases were completed during the period of research resulting in theoretical cost calculations. However, inflation adjusted comparisons with a 1998 LSC study[3] of lawyer costs suggested that mediation was cheaper – a case dealing with children issues cost £872 compared with an equivalent (1998) lawyer-handled case at £1,324. (Interestingly, the LSC 2003 average cost of mediation was cheaper at £738 per case.[4]) Did the research influence policy at all or was it in the end largely a means of satisfying public accountability?

Despite these trying times, Community Legal Service (CLS) contracts with local mediation services in both the not-for-profit and private sector were successfully set up and widely spread around the country. As mediation became accessible to all, mediators across the board were trained in every core requirement, both child-focused and all-issues mediation, together with cross-cultural practice and domestic violence screening. National mediator bodies in both sectors worked hard with the help of government project grants to equip their members for the changes. The UK College grew in scope, approving a number of new training bodies, overcoming initial tensions and trying to meet often unrealistic expectations with the help of a firm chair in Dame Margaret Booth and Elizabeth Walsh as chief executive, who also organised an impressive number of seminars around the

---

[1] Legal Services Commission Annual Report 2001/2.
[2] LSC Report on the Monitoring of publicly-funded mediation (2001).
[3] S Maclean, 'Report of the Case Profiling Study'. London: The Legal Services Commission (1998).
[4] Annual Report of the Legal Services Commission 2002/3.

country demonstrating mediation to local judges. Such a demonstration was further transported to Strasbourg to a European Conference in 1998, held to launch a recommendation to the Committee of Ministers that mediation should be developed and promoted.[1] There had never been, nor probably would be again, so many mediators working so hard at local and national level.

Competence assessment and standardising standards

The assessment of mediators was an urgent requirement of the CLS and a way of achieving this had to be found. The Mediation Forum had most recently widened its scope to embrace mediators in other fields. Part of building common ground had been the formulation of a generic account of the mediation process and skills initially based on the NFM skills list. This had led to an exercise in casting the process into the language and form of a National Vocational Qualification with the requisite assistance of government hired personnel skilled in the new discourse. When the urgent request came from the CLS, it was to the almost completed NVQ formula to which we turned. In a short space of time, this was converted into a competence assessment tool that required written accounts of recent cases by each mediator, both newly trained and very experienced. A supervisor had to submit an accompanying witness testimony. This challenged the habits of thought and practice of the entire mediator community and added new requirements to the role of the mediator supervisor or consultant – a role that the College had already determinedly and controversially imposed in order to have a quality check on its own standards of membership renewal.

The College had at this point to consider its role very carefully lest its functions were to be undermined by a government body which, if that were to amount to statutory regulation by the back door, would not apply to all mediators, but only to those who chose to do legally aided work. What was the optimum relationship between self-regulation and government regulation? Where should professional control of mediation properly reside? The College stood for the same standards expected of every mediator regardless of the income band of their clients, the profession from which they came or the sector within which they worked. The short-term solution had to look to a long-term future. The arrangement was reached that the College recruited assessors whose work was overseen by a qualified NVQ assessor and that the CLS managed the procedure. Eventually, the College was to carry out all these functions and the LSC would accept its judgments. The College would then, with some exceptions, make the same requirement of College members who did not carry out legally aided work. The College's early ambition to be the one professional body for family mediators was not, however, achievable as the Law Society concluded that it could not delegate the responsibility for those solicitors who mediated within their own practices. However, agreement was reached on harmonisation of standards and codes of practice. The government's eventual award of a quality mark for mediation (both community and family) put the stamp of approval at the end of a lengthy consultation process.

---

[1]   Recommendation No R (98) 1, Committee of Ministers to Member States on Family Mediation.

Part II of the Family Law Act

In July 1999, the Lord Chancellor decided not to implement Part II of the Family Law Act which would have changed the substantive divorce law and required the attendance of divorce petitioners at face-to-face information meetings. This had an immediate effect upon public confidence in mediation as the decision was presented by putting undue emphasis on the expectation that mediations would flow in far greater numbers than was realisable in the government run pilot. This was also a dramatic blow to those who had energetically developed and researched information meetings, including the regional structure created to support them which had been managed by the NCFP, chaired by Lord Justice Thorpe. With hindsight, these downturns in confidence proved to be temporary and other structures were set to arise in their place. The salient parts of the Family Law Act empowering the public funding of mediation were removed to the Access to Justice Act, the NCFP did not survive but a Family Justice Council is now about to be instituted and yet more experimentation in the delivery of information to divorcing individuals was to follow in the form of piloting a Family Advice and Information Service (FAINs).

Fourth phase: franchises and a framework for regulation (2000 to the present time)

How might we now view the current situation of the provision of family mediation and the effectiveness of regulating professional standards?

Mediation services

First, what we see is a network of 227 government franchised family mediation services in both the private and not-for-profit sectors and, as far as is known, nationwide provision of privately funded mediation. Mediators are supported by much smaller national bodies whose purpose and survival is in many ways as uncertain as in the development years.

Secondly, the cascade of newly trained mediators in the wake of the Family Law Act has become a small stream. An unknown number of mediators have stopped mediating, especially among solicitors as the legal aid fees in all areas of legal practice (not mediation in particular where the fees are not quite as low) are found by many firms to be insufficient. At the time of writing, legal aid fees to not-for-profit services are yet to be finally settled. Thirdly, the take-up of mediation in publicly funded work, which are the only mediations nationally counted, shows a year on year increase (12 per cent for 2002/3 over 2001/3 to 13,841 starts in mediation) which was shared in 2002 on a ratio of 5:4 between the private and not-for-profit sectors.[1] The body of work done by each mediator has undoubtedly increased which should have improved practice. The legal device (s 11 of the Access to Justice Act 1999) whereby mediators inform divorcing couples about mediation by mediators, although initially controversial and administratively complicated (involving solicitors sending legal aid clients first to mediator meetings) has been more effectively worked out and talk of its being discontinued

---

[1] Legal Services Commission Annual Report 2002/3.

is at least on hold. One might surmise that the market is settling down. During the passage of the Family Law Bill, Professor Cretney wrote that mediation should have been supported earlier in order to find its own place in the system. Is this now occurring?

Professional standards

The UK College of Family Mediators, administratively modest, performs its basic task of registering and renewing membership. The Law Society Family Mediation Panel has been launched. Neither system seems likely to subvert the other. The UK College journal which took over from the successful and long-running NFM Family Mediation Journal now combines with MediationUK to publish a quarterly journal entitled 'Mediation in Practice' which, with a College newsletter, is the current inheritor of the Conciliation Newsletter begun by Jack Chapman in 1983. The College continues to publish guidance on areas of practice which have the strength of approval by both sectors. For example, the widespread emphasis on professionals listening to the voice of the child has been reflected in continuing work on how mediators can incorporate this and the latest research into the effects of divorce on children[1,2] into their practice. There have been successful conferences in the last few years which have attracted mediators from north and south to hear speakers of standing and relevance. Meetings between mediation consultants on a regional basis appear to be developing and these add credence to the College regulatory systems. The College responds to public debate on mediation and divorce law issues through the commitment and experience of its governors. There will be a mediator on the new Family Justice Council and, although working relationships vary at local level between family solicitors, courts and members of the Children and Family Court Advisory and Support Service (CAFCASS), they are nationally maintained and will find formal channels through the Family Justice Council.

What is the future for collaboration between mediators across the areas?

Finally, is there any future for combining in some way, either in practice and/or in regulation, the whole profession of mediators regardless of their field of operation – family, community, civil, commercial, industrial or restorative justice? Many mediators now work in more than one field. MediationUK and the UK College held a successful joint Conference in 2003. NFM and MedUK have created a single organisation to represent mediation services in the not-for-profit sector to achieve economies of scale and better services to local providers and clients. Early attempts have been made to design an Institute of Conflict Resolution to bring together all areas of mediation in some way but until there is a practical or political imperative, experience suggests that progress will be slow. The important thing is that mediation now occurs in general conversations and its spread to other fields

---

[1]   C Smart and A Wade 'As fair as it can be? Childhood after divorce' in A Jensens and L McKee, *Children and the Changing Family: Between Transformation and Negotiation* (FalmerRoutledge, 2003), at pp 105–199.

[2]   C Smart, B Neale, and A Wade *The Changing Experience of Childhood: Families and Divorce*, (Cambridge, Polity, 2001).

illuminates its meaning in each field. It is, as was first hoped, a 'social practice' well attuned to the needs of a post-modern society where peaceful negotiation of disputes is increasingly sought.

Chapter 8

THE DEVELOPMENT OF THE ROLE OF THE FAMILY MEDIATOR

Kay Begg

In 1978 I undertook my first conciliation. It was held amongst the lingering atmosphere of tobacco in the borrowed board room of Bristol Council of Social Service, used the night before for an AA meeting. I can still remember the young couple, confused and deeply distressed. She wanted to leave the marriage, set up her own business and be independent. Was there someone else? They had a daughter of school age whom they both loved and cared for. Working out how they continued parenting together was not difficult for them, but fitting this into the legal slots of custody and care and control was. He did not want to separate and told me he loved her. I asked if he had told her. He then did. She cried and they left hand in hand. I remember not only because it was my first interview but also because 2 years later they returned to mediation.

Did I understand what I was doing as a mediator? I am not sure I did for I was drawing heavily on my training as a social worker and as a counsellor and still had unformed ideas of what mediation was, let alone how to manage it.

The team

We were a small group, all trained as social workers or marriage guidance counsellors, enthusiastic, bold, pioneers. We met in each other's homes to tease out, with the help of the little written material then available to us, what we were going to do as mediators. For the first months we worked, without pay or our own accommodation, seeing couples referred to us by a few equally enthusiastic local solicitors keen for us to set up a mediation service.

The Service proper was opened a year later in 1979 with a full-time job-sharing co-ordinator post, full-time secretary and three part-time mediators. After 10 months the job share changed to one full-time co-ordinator combining management with mediation practice. This pattern of management and practice for the co-ordinator post has continued until recently when these functions were divided and our present part-time manager, who is not a mediator, was appointed.

Our team has always been very small, reasoning that it was more efficient to have a few working, say 2 days a week, rather than more working for one or half a day. This has meant that we have each been able to build up a great deal of experience which was not possible in many other organisations offering mediation at the time. We rarely co-worked, and this is still the position; we usually saw each client separately first and then both together; a pattern that has been modified over the years.

We experimented. I remember trying to mediate on the phone with a husband in Switzerland and a wife in the office – not a good idea. We had clients from a wide spectrum of Bristol and further afield. We occasionally saw grandparents. We began to mediate between parents whose children were in care, and the local authority as the other parent, an area which has since been tried and researched by the Tavistock Institute in a combined project with National Family Mediation.

Development of practice and training

Looking back at some yellowing notes of those early years, it is clear that we worked hard and progressed rapidly. With the help of our supervisor, who was also making the transition from a therapeutic background to the new perspective of mediator, we set out our objectives and criteria for practice. That mediation should be neutral, confidential and voluntary with the clients being the decision-makers was always clear. So too were the goals to open up communication between the couple, being future focused and time limited. We decided that we would work with couples who were parents, whether married or separated or single-sex couples.

We knew that a main focus of our work would be children. We were a platform for the recommendations of the Finer Report[1] which had seen conciliation as 'reducing the area of conflict upon custody, support, access to and education of the children'. These were issues where many lawyers welcomed support, and where we with our social work consciences felt at home. It was by then being said that the adversarial system was not appropriate to deal with family matters because it was expensive and might make things worse.

From the beginning the mediators, all of whom had training and experience in addressing emotional relationships, were clear that mediation was different. Although its theoretical base is informed by 'the caring professions' and particularly many aspects of family therapy, it has been stressed over the years that mediation focuses on the negotiation and settlement of issues in dispute rather than on restructuring family relationships or counselling individuals.

To discuss such matters and enhance our practice, family mediators in the South West began to meet regularly. Other areas did the same encouraging the National Family Conciliation Council (later National Family Mediation) to set up a Regional Council to work alongside the national Management Committee. I became the first Regional Council chairman and thus began my close association with the national body. The regional structure has remained important. In the South West managers and coordinators meet to discuss management issues and exchange information on such matters as the latest Legal Services Commission's contracts. The supervisors also have a regional group and organise an annual training day.

---

[1] *The Finer Report on One-Parent Families* (1974).

In the early years, conferences and workshops locally and nationally, together with the appointment of a training officer, had been giving us training and the opportunity to share our ideas. However, it was not until 1986 that, following a stimulating national working weekend in Bristol, the NFCC's Core Training Programme was established.

Keeping to the process of mediation had become clearer with the Core Training Programme. It has provided structure and an explicit map of the mediation process to guide the mediator. The NFCC training also insisted on the integration of theory with the practice which mediators actually experienced.

Although our team held knowledge about family dynamics and children we were always clear that we were not child experts. We felt that we could not help children effectively without seeking to help the parents. Marital breakdown is a crisis often accompanied by confusion, always by distress, anger and a great sense of loss, particularly of children; and fear of loss fuels conflict. It became our principle that we would work primarily with parents, seeing children if both parents and the children agreed, and with the same confidentiality given to each one of them; never as an advocate for one or other of their parents. This principle holds good for BFM today. Disputes focused on access, care and control and custody of children, now called 'contact and residence'. Many parents did not really understand what these different categories meant.

The changes brought with the arrival in 1989 of the Children Act were very welcome. For family mediation the new clarity in terminology was particularly helpful. Previously there had been slight overtones of children as packages to be moved about which was thankfully no longer there. The principle that no order for the care of children would be made unless the parents were unable to agree arrangements, gave the message that parents were competent to work plans out themselves. This they often did with the help of a mediator.

Outside interest

We began to be known more widely and clients would travel to see us. There was publicity on the radio, television and in newspapers. We would be asked to provide clients willing to be interviewed. This was a dilemma: we wanted more and more couples to learn about family mediation, but we were very clear that it was not appropriate to expose people to the glare of the media whilst they were actively going through mediation. We did role plays for TV and the backs of our heads were sometimes seen on TV screens. The media issues demonstrated the value of the National Family Conciliation Council which provided written guidelines for its increasing number of affiliated services and would also often handle those persistent journalists.

Our raised profile attracted many visitors from this country and overseas. Other mediators in training spent time with us to increase their experience and regional groups of mediators began to meet regularly to share practice and management issues.

Money concerns were always a shadow over us and we were on the point of closure several times.

National Family Conciliation Council / National Family Mediation

The Bristol Service has played an active part in establishing and running the National Family Conciliation Council, later called National Family Mediation. Different members of the Service have taken part in working groups, and were prominent in the national Management Committee. In these ways BFM has helped to formulate policy and practice for mediation. The NFM procedures for the selection, training and accreditation as a mediator were all established with input from the Bristol Service. It always felt very important to me that we were mediation practitioners and that any contributions I made to NFM sprang from these experiences.

Our Service has always had the help of a supervisor who has provided support, creative input and accountability for mediation practice in the Service. Our Service assisted NFM to develop skills and training for supervision and has provided supervisors from among its mediators for other NFM Services. Supervision is a key role for mediation. It is used to assess mediators in the competence assessment procedure, it forms the gateway to membership of the UK College of Family Mediators and the supervisory process has been adopted by the Legal Services Commission as a key component in monitoring the standards of practising mediators.

Research

Family Conciliation – 'It All Boils Down to Personalities, Doesn't It?'[1] This strange title was used by the University of Newcastle Conciliation Project Unit to present to BFM, at their 10th Anniversary Conference. It focused on the findings of the research they had carried out between 1985 and 1989 into court-based conciliation and that provided by independent conciliation. This anniversary was an exciting day for us, for despite repeated struggles over funding, here we were, the largest and longest established independent family mediation service in the country.

The research, which was looking at 'the cost and effectiveness of family mediation', was very gratifying to us, for it showed a high level of client satisfaction. Almost 90 per cent of service users said they would recommend the service to others and over 80 per cent reported that they had found their conciliator helpful. Indeed, the conciliators were described in complimentary terms as 'calm, patient, easy to relate to, non-judgmental, helpful, sympathetic, neutral, under-standing, intelligent, level-headed, professional, competent and normal'.

That we were all female was criticised; during the next decade, we rectified this. Not only was it difficult to find men willing to work part-time and for the money

---

[1]   J Walker, J Corlyon and R Simpson 'Family Conciliation – It All Boils Down to Personalities. A Study of the Bristol Family Conciliation Service' (Conciliation Project Unit, University of Newcastle).

we were paid then, but equal opportunities had not become to the fore as it did later.

Clients were shown to be particularly appreciative of single appointments preceding joint ones, which someone described as 'better than going in cold'. Equally appreciated was the space allowed to parties to express their fears about the future; this was seen as instrumental in allowing a compromise to be reached, and in clarifying points which one party might have misunderstood.

The report's recommendations for the future included factors which it was felt could effectively hinder conciliation. I am writing them out in full because they remain just as relevant today as they did then:

(a) it should not be mandatory for all couples;
(b) it should not focus exclusively on child issues;
(c) it should not overlap with other legal and welfare processes.

For effectiveness to be maximised, the researchers believed that:

(d) conciliation should be recognised as an alternative mechanism to legal, adjudicatory procedures for the resolution of disputes and be identifiable as a discrete, unambiguous process;
(e) its distinguishing feature should be to enable couples to retain control of the decision-making process contingent on separation and divorce, encouraging them to reach their own agreements;
(f) the arena in which it takes place should be conducive to civilised discussion with an appropriate degree of informality.

The report went on to say that 'our research suggests that there should be standardisation of processes and that the terminology should be more uniform and less ambiguous. In principle, finance and property issues should not be excluded from the remit of a conciliation service'.

In this last paragraph in particular, lie the beginnings of two very important developments for BFM which were to emerge in the next decade – All Issues Mediation and the UK College of Family Mediators. Both these developments illustrate the shift to the term 'mediation' in place of 'conciliation' which was less prone to confusion, especially 'conciliation' with 'reconciliation', and confirmed the adoption of the term throughout the UK.

All Issues Mediation

The first of these developments, All Issues Mediation, had been heralded by the Finer Report in 1974. The Report had seen conciliation as not only dealing with the consequences of the breakdown of marriages and disputes over children, but had gone on to say that it should consider 'financial provision, disposition of the matrimonial home ... and every other matter arising from the breakdown which calls for a decision on future arrangements'. Mediators at BFM had been highlighting for some years the difficulties of dealing with divorce and children issues without being able to adequately explore questions about finance and property.

Lawyers, in particular, were somewhat alarmed at the thought of mediators, untrained legally, dealing in these matters, and it is fair to say very concerned as to where the boundaries of mediation should be drawn and the effect on their practices. There were anxious lawyers among the Trustees of BFM, echoing the reactions of the Law Society.

However, the move towards mediation including issues of finance and property was gaining ground. Solicitors in Mediation, the forerunner of the Family Mediators Association, were showing what could be done, and by 1990 the NFCC Comprehensive Mediation Project funded by the Joseph Rowntree Foundation began. The 2½-year project aimed to develop comprehensive mediation in five NFCC Services, and to make it available to those on low or moderate income. The development work of these five Services, each using slightly different models from each other, was to be researched by an academic team led by Janet Walker at Newcastle University.[1]

In the Bristol model we were to have a lawyer, trained as a mediator, joining the mediation process at certain defined points during the mediation process. Three solicitors and a barrister joined the Service to become lawyer mediators. The mediators and the lawyers taking part were sent for training together where we met the charismatic John Haines who became such a friend and guru for many of us. Could mediators carry out the comprehensive mediation process? How could legal and financial expertise be appropriately included? How could full disclosure be ensured? Would the focus on children be affected? How long would it take? and What would it cost? were only some of the questions.

The NFCC report[2] on the project 3 years later found answers as follows. Not only could the Service's non-lawyer mediators conduct mediation on finance and property, but they became enthusiastic about the process and about interdisciplinary teams. All the five different models within the project were successful in introducing legal and financial information into the process, and it was found that the model was less important than the conduct of the process. The information gathering procedures were effective in ensuring full disclosure. The focus on the children was not obscured and planning for the future needs of children was more thorough in that it covered all aspects of their care – financial support and housing as well as contact and residence.

Working with lawyer mediators

Working with our lawyer colleagues was stimulating. I remember too that it had its moments of stress. Court timetables did not consult with BFM's needs, and

---

[1]   J Walker, P McCarthy and N Timms, *Mediation: The Making and Remaking of Cooperative Relationships. An Evaluation of the Effectiveness of Comprehensive Mediation* (Relate Centre for Family Studies, University of Newcastle, March 1994).

[2]   *The National Association of Family Mediation and Conciliation Services Comprehensive Mediation Project Report 1994.*

sometimes our lawyers found themselves, at short notice, in Weston or even Bodmin, when we expected them beside us in Bristol.

Although I am one of the first to say that the process of mediation is all important and that procedure and context come after, I would not want to underestimate how much the mediators had to learn about matrimonial law and finance and property, or the lawyers about family dynamics. Many of us were surprised to find that from then on we would turn to the financial pages of newspapers and journals with enthusiasm and alacrity.

Mediation is not merely a hybrid activity made up from the existing professional knowledge and experience of lawyers and therapists. It would be unwise to ignore the importance that the knowledge from these different backgrounds can bring, and the influence of each profession learning from the other as well as from the generic process of mediation.

Mediation training now includes teaching on the principles of family law and child development. Mediators need to be informed and to know the legal parameters but most importantly to make sure couples obtain advice from the experts outside the mediation. It is widely recognised that one of the most difficult parts of mediation training is to leave behind, without abandoning, one's pre-mediation background, especially where it had a strong focus on advising, and instead create the environment for clients to make their own informed decisions. In the early days I have watched my much respected lawyer mediator colleagues barely able to contain themselves from putting forward a neat solution to a financial problem with helpful advice on the suitability of a Mesher order perhaps, or whether to sell the matrimonial home! Similarly, mediators with a social work or counselling background have to restrain themselves from exploring in detail a client's barely suppressed anger or a deep-seated bereavement issue. It is very frustrating to be a knowledgeable lawyer and not give advice, or to be an experienced therapist and not try to explore the couples' personalities.

There is a quote from a family solicitor in the research on Comprehensive Mediation which sums it up.

'I think when I started I had a very vague idea of it being something like a holiday from being a solicitor for a while. Now it feels very much more that it is as difficult if not more difficult than being a solicitor. But a different job. Different things being important.'[1]

It is interesting to add that the NFCC selection procedure had brought recognition that you do not have to be a counsellor or lawyer to be a competent family mediator, and mediators today come from varied backgrounds.

---

[1]   J Walker, P McCarthy and N Timms, *Mediation: The Making and Remaking of Cooperative Relationships. An Evaluation of the Effectiveness of Compehensive Mediation* (Relate Centre for Family Studies, University of Newcastle, March 1994).

The UK College of Family Mediators

As mediation was becoming increasingly well known and attractive to would-be practitioners, there was an increasing and urgent need to establish a single regulatory body of family mediators which would set and maintain professional standards for all those practising family mediation. This would not only protect the public by ensuring that they can have access to properly trained and experienced mediators, but would also regulate the provision of training.

The UK College of Family Mediators was launched in January 1996 with three parent bodies: National Family Mediation, Family Mediators Association and Family Mediation Scotland. At the end of a 3-year period the membership was widened to include further bodies which met the standards for training and practice; there are now five such Approved Bodies represented on the College Board of Governors. The College publishes a directory of qualified family mediators who meet the standards required for membership of the College. All the Bristol Service mediators are on this list.

Bristol, again, was in evidence in setting up the College. The Vice-Chair of the Governors came from the Bristol Service, and two of our lawyers generously wrote several chapters for the College Directory and Handbook. As the regulator of mediator standards, it has made manifest sense for the College to take over the Competence Assessment of all family mediators from the Legal Services Commission. It has also honed the criteria and framework for, among other things, Professional Practice Consultancy/Supervision with a paper setting out the roles and responsibilities for Professional Practice Consultants. This is a move I greatly welcome and I look forward to a sharing of these responsibilities across the Approved Bodies. The College has also clearly filled a mediator need by creating excellent AGMs combined with a lively conference. Long may these continue.

It is an irony that, after many years of travelling up and down to London for NFM and College meetings, both these organisations have now moved to Bristol!

The Bristol team still remains small and efficient. There are five part-time mediators with a mix of social work, probation and solicitor backgrounds. The amount of administration and paperwork has increased greatly with the arrival of Legal Services Commission Contracts. The Service could not function without the support of the service manager, together with the administrative staff. The increase in financial and administrative work is reflected by this book containing a full chapter on funding the local family mediation service!

The team is still bold, having been submitted to more research, this time 'Monitoring Publicly Funded Family Mediation', a report directed by Gwynn Davis for the Legal Service Commission. It is still pioneering and over the last year two mediators from the present team have been involved in a pilot project in collaboration with Local Authority Housing Departments seeking to reduce the number of young people going into temporary accommodation as a result of parental evictions. Again we were pioneering as BFM is one of the first family mediation services to try this.

As I have been writing, I have made a list of some of the things that I believe have been particularly important to me in my family mediator life. In no particular order they are:

–   the importance of language and of the choice of words in creating a decision-making atmosphere;
–   establishing communication and rapport with clients;
–   the importance of the first four minutes of an interview;
–   taking control of the process of an interview but not the decisions;
–   always asking questions and thus avoiding making statements;
–   being future focused.

It is the skill with which the mediation process is conducted that matters, rather than whether one co-works, or sole works, or sees clients separately or only together and so on. There are different theories and styles of practice, the use of systems theory for example or more recently transformative mediation. These have and are playing a part in the practice of mediation. Over the years I have been able to try elements of a number of them. However, what remains important in my mind is following the basic process and stages of mediation: establishing the arena, clarifying the issues, exploring the issues, developing the options, securing agreement. These are the golden mean.

To sum up, the mediator's role is to provide a neutral forum for rational discussion which is emotionally and ethically safe, and follows the process of mediation throughout. BFM mediators have always been working to this goal. I can now stand back and say that I am immensely proud to have been one of them.

Chapter 9

FROM SERVICE TO SUPPLIER: FUNDING 'NOT-FOR-PROFIT' FAMILY MEDIATION SERVICE

Trevor Morkham

The Bristol Service's annual accounts for April 1990, just 6 months before I began my tenure as manager, make interesting reading even for those whose eyes tend to glaze over at the sight of a well-turned balance sheet. In that year, the Service boasted a total income of just over £40,000, of which the greater part – around £35,000, or more than 80 per cent – came from charitable trusts or fundraising activities of some kind. By contrast, only about £5,500 (13 per cent) was generated by the client-based work, itself more-or-less equally divided between client 'donations' (we were not allowed to call them fees) and the modest amount claimed from the Legal Aid Board (as it was then known) via the clients' solicitors under the device known as the Green Form extension.

The Legal Aid Board had consistently maintained that it could not provide direct financial support for mediation as this would have been deemed to be ultra vires. However, following some persuasive lobbying from the Service in the early 1980s, the Board agreed that where a mediation client was already in receipt of legal aid under the so-called Green Form scheme, the client's solicitor could apply for an extension to the Green Form to pay for the report or summary letter sent by the Service at the conclusion of mediation. Clients who did not have the benefit of legal aid, usually because they were either financially ineligible or unrepresented, would be invited by the mediator to make a one-off payment of £25 towards the cost of their mediation; although it was always emphasised that this was a 'voluntary' contribution and that no client would be refused mediation on the grounds of their inability – so, by implication, unwillingness – to pay.

The accounts for April 1990 also indicate that the Service's total overheads (for staff, premises, administration and so on) amounted to a little over £20,000, representing less than half its income for the year. Not bad going, considering the Service's status as a not-for-profit organisation! As is often the way, of course, these accounts are notable as much for what they hide as for what they reveal. Most importantly, they do not include the salary costs for the manager and for all except one of the mediators, who at that stage were on the Avon Probation payroll and therefore technically seconded to the Bristol Service. If the cost of employing these staff had been included in the Service's overheads, the figure would have been nearer £50,000, turning the apparent surplus of £20,000 into a £10,000 deficit.

The Bristol Service was not alone in being substantially funded by the 'back door' at this time. Many conciliation/mediation services received similar help from local statutory or voluntary bodies through the provision of staff, premises or other support in kind. With BFM, as with so many others, this had the dual effect of enabling the Service to continue functioning whilst at the same time disguising the real cost of sustaining it.

More insidiously, the Service's dependence on a combination of periodic crisis appeals and the continued beneficence of Avon Probation – which together contributed around 90 per cent of the annual running costs – left BFM extremely vulnerable to the whims of changing fashion on the part of funding charities and to shifts in policy and priorities within the statutory agencies. Over the ensuing years, the progressive reduction in financial support from Avon Probation – culminating in complete withdrawal in 1999 – combined with the increasingly difficult task of persuading charities and trusts to part with money for a service which they regarded as the responsibility of government to finance, convinced the Trustees that the Service should set itself the goal of achieving a position of self-sufficiency as soon as possible.

A scrutiny of the accounts for the later years of the 1990s shows that by the end of the decade the Service could justifiably claim to have achieved that financial Holy Grail, namely a more-or-less balanced budget from one year to the next. Just as important was the fact that by this stage almost 90 per cent of its total income was being generated by client-based activities. The story of how this was achieved by BFM to a greater or lesser extent mirrors the journey undertaken by many mediation services in the not-for-profit sector over this period.

Changing the culture

For an understanding of how this transition took place, it is necessary to begin with the people at the heart of the process, namely the mediators. In common with most other not-for-profit services, BFM had from the outset tended to recruit its mediators from amongst a fairly narrow range of practitioners already working within the so-called 'helping' professions, notably social workers, Court Welfare Officers and counsellors. In the early years the primary focus of mediation was on disputes over children, mostly around what we now call Contact and Residence, and so not surprisingly the Service looked towards those who might be expected to have a sound grasp of family dynamics and of the issues of family breakdown, together with experience of working with families or couples in crisis. Then, as now, the emphasis was on mediation as an *alternative* to the court process, rather than an adjunct to it, and therefore knowledge of family law or of court procedures in relation to family matters was not generally regarded as a pre-requisite to becoming a mediator – advantageous, certainly, but not essential. Hence it was relatively unusual at that time for the not-for-profit services to draw their mediators from the legal profession, for example; indeed there was a body of opinion in some mediation circles that lawyers, by the very nature of their training and practice, were generally unsuited to be mediators at all.

One of the main consequences of this recruitment policy for mediation services like BFM was that even until well into the 1990s it was predominantly staffed by mediators whose previous work experience was in the statutory or voluntary sector and whose familiarity with the commercial world was, to say the least, limited. They were people who were politically and philosophically committed to the principle of public service and of service provision being based on need rather than on the ability to pay. The very idea of charging an economic rate for mediation and of collecting payments from clients on this basis would have been regarded as unacceptable, even anathema, to most mediators.

More than anything else, it was the selection of BFM as one of the five local services to be involved in the pioneering of Comprehensive (later All Issues) Mediation at the beginning of the 1990s which marked the turning point in mediator attitudes within BFM. First, the decision to recruit lawyer-mediators to work alongside the Service's 'indigenous' staff on AIM (All Issues Mediation) cases soon began to impact on the cultural homogeneity which had existed within the staff group up to that point. Secondly, the position on AIM adopted by the Trustees, who took the view that this new project had to be self-financing and could not be subsidised from the Service's general funds, meant that the mediators found themselves having to ask AIM clients to pay up front for the full cost, which could amount to ten times what they had been used to seeking by way of a 'donation'. At the same time, mediators were inevitably seeing in some detail their clients' financial circumstances and were therefore often acutely aware both of what the clients could afford to pay and of how much those same clients stood to save by using mediation rather than by going down the traditional solicitor-led adversarial route. Mediators came to appreciate the increasingly symbiotic relationship between the income they were able to generate from their work with clients and the Service's capacity to continue to function. Equally importantly, mediators who had previously perceived their work with clients primarily in terms of its social value now began to also assess it in respect of its *financial* benefits to the clients and to the public purse.

Alongside the change in attitude taking place on the part of the mediators, there was also a perceptible and comparable shift in thinking amongst the Trustees. There had always been a strong emphasis on the importance of providing a high quality service, and the decision taken at the outset to employ the mediators on a salaried basis, which until relatively recently was still almost unique to BFM, was viewed by the Trustees as evidence of their commitment to that ideal. The prevailing belief was that so long as BFM and its fellow services in the National Family Mediation network continued to demonstrate the value of their contribution to families experiencing separation or divorce, sooner or later the Government would have to step in to provide more permanent and reliable funding. As the decade progressed, however, the Trustees came to realise that even if Government funding were eventually to be forthcoming, some degree of private income generation would probably be essential for the Service to be able to survive in the long term. There was a subtle change in the terminology employed by the Trustees during this period which is itself quite revealing; from being concerned with a 'service' which needed to be 'promoted', they began to refer to the 'product' which needed to be 'marketed', and even went so far as to commission an independent report from a commercial marketing organisation. The decision by the Trustees to incorporate, which came into effect in January 1997, reconstituted BFM as a limited company run by a small Board of Directors and in retrospect can be seen as a timely restructuring given what lay around the corner.

Family Law Act – a watershed

All these factors taken together served to place the Bristol Service in a relatively strong position to accommodate the radical changes to its funding which followed on from the passing of the Family Law Act in 1996. It is fair to say that the atmosphere of optimism and even euphoria in the mediation world which accompanied the advent of divorce reform and public funding for mediation was tempered by serious reservations, in the not-for-profit sector at least, with the decision to channel that funding exclusively through the Legal Aid system. In particular, we were acutely aware of the climate of disaffection within the legal profession towards the Legal Aid Board and its implementation of legal aid in relation to family law, both in respect of the perception of excessive bureaucracy and inadequate levels of payment. Such concerns, however, were put firmly to the back of our minds as we sought to ensure that the Bristol Service was one of those selected for participation in Phase I of the Legal Aid Board's Mediation Pilot Project scheduled to commence in the summer of 1997. Having not long previously endured yet another funding crisis during which the spectre of closure had loomed as a very real possibility, the Trustees consequently viewed selection for Phase I as not just desirable but indeed essential for the Service's survival.

Happily our bid was successful, at which point we began the process of negotiating our contract with the Board. This proved to be a highly educational experience for me as I tried to get to grips with what seemed to be an arcane method of calculating the payments to be made to the Service. We were required to supply the Board with a detailed projection of all the mediation-related work we expected to carry out over the following 12 months, including a breakdown of the numbers of publicly funded and private paying clients anticipated for each type of case (Children Issues, Finance and Property, and All Issues Mediation). We were also expected to provide precise costings for each of these areas of work. With little idea what impact the introduction of public funding would have on the take-up of mediation, and even less as to the proportion of our clients who would actually qualify for such funding, the figures we eventually submitted to the Board owed rather more to inspired guesswork than scientific calculation. Amazingly, when the time came to renegotiate our contract under Phase II the following year, our projections turned out to have been uncannily accurate. With experience it has become progressively easier to forecast these figures with a degree of confidence and precision. Nevertheless, such predictions can never be entirely reliable, not least because of the vagaries of external circumstances over which the Service has no control (such as the emergence of a new competitor with a contract to provide publicly funded mediation).

Having bitten the bullet and committed the Service to participation in Phase I of the Pilot Project, no one involved with BFM was under any illusions about the fact that we had effectively gone past the point of no return. It was not long before our early misgivings about the suitability of the Legal Aid Board to manage the Project re-emerged with the Board's announcement that all mediators conducting publicly funded mediation would be required to undergo an NVQ based assessment of their competence to practise. We understood, of course, that the political constraints under which the Board operated required it to be accountable for the use of public funds. However, for those mediators who had already accumulated many years of mediation experience, the requirement to prove their competence at all, never mind submit themselves to the same assessment process as someone who may have only recently trained, was deeply resented by some.

It gradually became apparent that the Legal Aid Board's determination to get the Competence Assessment programme up and running was driven by increasing political pressure to bring s 29 of the Family Law Act into play. The implementation of s 29 was in turn seen by the Board as critical to its efforts to increase the overall take-up of mediation, since this provision introduced a statutory requirement on solicitors to refer their clients to a local mediation supplier for an assessment as to 'suitability' for mediation before any application could be made for a full Legal Aid Certificate. The Board contended that if members of the public were in effect to be compelled to attend for interview in order to 'consider' mediation – even though the decision whether to proceed with mediation itself was still voluntary – clients were entitled to be assured that *any* mediator with whom they might come into contact had attained a minimum standard of competence to practise. In the event, central Bristol was one of only two areas in the country – the other being Northampton – selected to pilot the introduction of s 29 in March 1998. For a few brief months, until other areas began to be brought under the remit of this section of the Act, BFM had the distinction of being the only not-for-profit Service licensed by the Legal Aid Board to take referrals for All Issues Mediation under s 29.

Subsequently re-invented as section 11 of the Funding Code, s 29 has encountered a good deal of hostility amongst the legal profession where it is viewed principally as a bureaucratic irritant and an unnecessary obstacle to the processing of public funding (legal aid) applications. Amongst mediators it is regarded as something of a curate's egg. It has undoubtedly led to an upturn in referrals, which in turn has resulted in a corresponding increase both in the number of 'assessment' interviews designed to pave the way for mediation and in the administrative procedure referred to as the Willingness Test which is intended to sound out potential takers for mediation. In each case, the work attracts a payment from public funds even where no mediation actually follows. If the experience of BFM is typical, however, it is by no means apparent that this measure has had a significant impact on the overall volume of mediations undertaken. On the other hand, there is no doubt in my mind that it has been instrumental in breaking down the barrier which previously existed on the part of many solicitors towards referring clients for mediation on finance and property matters. It is surely no coincidence that the proportion of cases involving mediation on finance and property undertaken by BFM, representing less than 20 per cent of the total caseload in 1997, had mushroomed to almost 60 per cent within 3 years of s 29 coming into force.

For the benefit of the clients

Just as the Competence Assessment procedure was intended by the Legal Aid Board to establish a benchmark for the practice of individual mediators, so the Board also initiated a programme of Quality Assurance audits designed to bring suppliers' internal procedures in line with those already required of franchised legal firms. A major part of the preparation for the audit involved the creation of an Office Manual which, although an onerous undertaking initially, was undoubtedly beneficial in bringing together and formalising a great deal of resource and procedural information previously scattered about the organisation. Rather less welcome, at least to the mediators, was the introduction of audits for client files based on 'Transaction Criteria' similar to those used in the auditing of solicitors' files. Whilst it could be argued that this process led to some improvement in mediators' file recording practice as well as a degree of standardisation in the content of what was actually recorded, mediators generally regarded the 'tick box' approach adopted by the Board as tedious, excessively bureaucratic and of questionable value to the client.

Collectively these measures were meant to ensure a guaranteed standard of service to those clients receiving legally aided (publicly funded) mediation. However, there was, by definition, no equivalent protection envisaged for private paying clients, although the assumption was that such clients would nevertheless enjoy the same benefits by virtue of the standards being applied by the 'supplier' throughout its service delivery. Whilst not an unreasonable assumption in itself, it entirely side-stepped the issue of the protection – or lack of it – afforded to clients of mediation services which did not have a franchise to provide publicly funded mediation.

This was by no means the only inherent contradiction embodied in the Legal Aid Board's approach to the funding of mediation. For example, throughout the process of contracting with the not-for-profit services, the Board made it clear that its calculations were based on the assumption that all pre-existing funding, whether from charitable trusts, service level agreements or the like, would continue unaffected. Yet the decision by Avon Probation to drastically cut back on its financial support for BFM, taken just a few months after we signed our contract with the Legal Aid Board, exposed the naivety of this proposition which was subsequently quietly abandoned.

Another important ideological component of the Board's approach to public funding for mediation was the commitment to create a 'mixed economy' of providers located within the private and the not-for-profit sector. The rationale for this approach seemed to be derived partly from the experimental nature of the Pilot Project and the Board's understandable desire to obtain data from as wide a variety of supplier types as possible, and in part from the government's ideological commitment to promote 'consumer choice'. The direct consequence, in Bristol as in many other areas, was to pit local suppliers in competition with one another within a market which was still relatively small – (traditionally, the take up of mediation has tended to hover consistently at a figure equivalent to 10 per cent of the divorcing population) – when what was needed was a real incentive for suppliers to co-operate with each other in encouraging a greater awareness of, and willingness to use, mediation within the local community. For services in the not-for-profit sector, whose charitable status requires a degree of transparency through the publication of annual accounts, the production of an annual report and usually the staging of an open AGM, the effort to build a market share in competition with suppliers who are under no such obligation can sometimes seem like an unequal and unfair struggle. When the not-for-profit service also has to contend with other suppliers joining together in a cartel to cross-refer and effectively 'carve up' the local market, as has happened in some parts of the country (though not, so far as I am aware, in Bristol), the much-vaunted virtues of competition can seem rather elusive.

For all its shortcomings, the Legal Aid Board (now reincarnated as the Legal Services Commission) has undeniably played a major part in a process which has seen the Bristol Service experience a fourfold increase in 'turnover', from £40,000 in the year I became manager to its current level of £160,000. Along the way it has transformed itself from a hand-to-mouth Cinderella operation, dependent for its survival upon liberal helpings of goodwill and a judicious use of the begging bowl, to one whose funding base and financial management procedures are probably not that dissimilar from any number of other successful small businesses – including, no doubt, its mediation competitors in and around Bristol.

Whither BFM?

As always, the future continues to pose questions for Bristol Family Mediation and there is never a shortage of challenges for it to face. The annual battle to balance the budget, like the battle between Good and Evil, seems to be eternal; but it is one likely to be brought into sharper focus in October 2004 when the Legal Services Commission implements its fixed price contracts for mediation suppliers, part of the purpose of which is to link the money paid for publicly funded clients more closely to the work actually done as well as to recognise and reward 'successful' mediation. The prospect of substantial reductions in LSC funding which could accompany the new contracts has highlighted the extent to which BFM has become dependent on this revenue (currently representing around three-quarters of all the Service's income), and has intensified the search for alternative funding streams. The mantra of the moment, it seems, is Diversification, Diversification, Diversification!

Meanwhile the slow but methodical rolling out of the experimental FAINs project (Family Advice and Information Services), though it has yet to reach Bristol, could provide an opportunity for BFM to take a step closer to becoming the kind of 'one stop shop' which has been the aspiration of many of us over the years. In its wake, however, the accompanying loss of the s 29 (Funding Code) referrals from local solicitors, exacerbated by the alarming exodus of family lawyers from publicly funded work, will once again force the Service to look closely at its whole marketing strategy.

It is here, I believe, that perhaps the ultimate challenge lies for BFM and for other not-for-profit services. Having finally recognised the impossibility of continuing to cling to the ideal that mediation should be accessible to all, regardless of ability to pay (since the Service does not have the funds to subsidise clients on low incomes who do not qualify for publicly funded mediation), BFM's Directors are now obliged to pursue a businesslike approach, which means first and foremost concentrating the Service's efforts on those areas of activity which will maximise its income. Whether that can be achieved without sacrificing the commitment to provide a service which is concerned to respond to client need, and yet still balance the books, remains to be seen.

Chapter 10

THE FUTURE OF FAMILY MEDIATION

Elizabeth Walsh

The future is holistic

Timing is everything. This chapter was written in May 2004. In June and July 2004 we anticipate a Department of Constitutional Affairs (DCA) green paper on family relationships and a Legal Services Commission (LSC) consultation paper on the Funding Code. Some of this chapter is taken up with predicting what will be contained in those papers – both well pored over and interpreted by the time this book is published in October 2004. What are my qualifications for this crystal ball exercise? As well as being editor of *Family Law* and *International Family Law*, I am a family mediator in the Thames Valley area and set up a 'not-for-profit' service in my home town in 1996. I chair the local family proceedings court and from 1997–99 was Chief Executive of the UK College of Family Mediators. In 1997 I wrote a book *Working in the Family Justice System* (Jordans) which will have a second edition when I find the time.

Where will family mediation sit in these rapidly changing times? Marriage and divorce have to be seen against a backdrop of increasing cohabitation, delayed parenting, lone parenthood and living alone. Many more people than in the past experience a number of different family formations and family transitions throughout their adult lives. The decline in the number of marriages, and later marriage, does not necessarily mean a decline in partnership formation. The most recent research evidence, *Family Formation and Dissolution: Trends and Attitudes Among the Scottish Population*, published by the Scottish Executive Legal Studies Research Team in 2004, suggests that cohabiting couples either marry or split up within a relatively short time but even though cohabitation may be short-lived, increasing numbers of people are living in cohabitation at some stage in their lives, with a relatively higher level of cohabitation among younger people. This report led to the Scottish Executive, way ahead of the rest of the UK, putting forward in May 2004 firm proposals to reduce the periods of separation constituting 'grounds' for divorce from 5 years without consent to 2 years and from 2 years with consent to 1 year: 'to lessen the acrimony associated with fault-based divorces and enable couples who were determined to end their marriage to do so without unnecessary conflict and recrimination and allow parents and children to move on'. It also proposed financial legal safeguards for cohabiting couples.

The future of family mediation would have been a rather short chapter at the end of 2003 – more of the same story of resources, regulation, referrals and, dare I say, rivalries. The year 2004 has, however, seen a thrust in the alternative dispute resolution (ADR) movement which could draw the concept of 'mediate don't litigate' into public consciousness – a conclusion which was merely a vision 20, if not 10, years ago. For example:

(1)   In April 2004 a free advice service to encourage people to settle civil disputes out of court was set up by the DCA at Manchester County Court.

(2)   In March 2004 a DCA mediation pilot in relation to automatic mediation referrals was launched at the Central London Civil Justice Centre. About 20 cases a week are randomly selected at allocation. If parties object they risk liability for costs under Civil Procedure Rule 44.

(3)   In December 2003 the DCA introduced two new pre-action protocols, one covering disputes about housing disrepair, and the other illness and disease (ie personal injury claims not the result of an accident). The protocol stresses the importance of:
    –   sharing information at an early stage;
    –   attempting to negotiate a solution before beginning litigation;
    –   considering ADR (in particular ombudsman schemes) as a means of resolving disputes.

(4)   In February 2004 the Department for Trade and Industry published research, commissioned from the National Consumer Council, into ADR options in consumer disputes, identifying key areas which needed to be addressed, such as:
    –   improved consumer and adviser awareness and understanding of ADR;
    –   clearer definition of the status of ADR outcomes;
    –   easier enforceability of ADR agreements.

(5)   In February 2004 the Financial Services Authority extended the scope of its mediation scheme to all investigations except those involving criminal charges.

(6)   In February 2004 the National Council for Voluntary Organisations (NCVO) published a guide for voluntary organisations on dealing with disputes, and the potential value of mediation in resolving them. NCVO works with the Centre for Effective Dispute Resolution (CEDR) to provide a subsidised mediation service for the voluntary and community sector, funded by the Active Community Unit.

(7)   In December 2004 Oftel approved in principle a new dispute resolution scheme, covering Orange, Telewest, T-Mobile and some members of the Internet Service Providers Association including AOL and Freeserve. The Communications and Internet Services Adjudication Scheme (CISAS), will be administered by the Chartered Institute of Arbitrators.

(8)   The new Employment Act 2002 provides for regulations which will introduce fixed periods for conciliation in employment tribunal claims. The Government's aim is to influence parties so that they prioritise conciliation at the beginning of the process, with the hope that claims will be resolved earlier, and unnecessary ACAS tribunal applications will not be made.

(9)   The Chief Medical Officer published a consultation paper in 2003 dealing with clinical negligence disputes. *Making Amends* recommends making litigation a last resort in such disputes. This is in line with the DCA's public service agreement target 3, to reduce the proportion of disputes which have to be resolved by recourse to the courts. The LSC's response was that

'encouragement' had not been enough, and it needed to consult about introducing further degrees of compulsion at least to explore the possibility of mediation or to set benchmarks for the proportion of cases it would expect suppliers to mediate.

(10)　The Government aims to facilitate further use of restorative justice, where a facilitator brings together perpetrator and victim in order for the offender to make reparation either to the victim or the wider community. The first independent evaluation of Home Office funded crime reduction programme pilots was planned for Autumn 2004 with a final report in 2007. The Government is also funding a new diversionary restorative justice pilot due at the end of 2004.

To have a view of the future of family mediation we have to look not only at the future of ADR but also the future of advice-giving in the community. For example, an LSC pilot for a salaried scheme for publicly funded criminal defence lawyers has been up and running for some time and in May 2004 the DCA published a draft Criminal Defence Service Bill together with a consultation paper covering proposals for restructuring the criminal legal aid scheme, together with a stern warning that: 'it is worth emphasising that the impetus behind the Bill is not only the need to halt the rising costs associated with criminal legal aid, but also to prevent further erosion into the civil legal aid budget. Any cuts that may have to be made into the civil budget will have serious implications for the wider fight against social exclusion'. On the same day the DCA published *Legal and Advice Services – A Pathway to Regeneration* – a report on the role of legal and advice services in reducing social exclusion. The DCA also announced that it had started work on a fundamental legal aid review which will address how legal aid could best meet the needs of society.

The DCA/LSC family justice strategy

The LSC Funding Code consultation paper and the DCA green paper should by now be old news. What was the Government strategy leading to those publications? At the end of 2003, following a Cabinet reshuffle, there was a shift in responsibility for families and children to the Department for Education and Skills (DfES). Margaret Hodge was appointed the Minister of State for Children, in a new Directorate for Children and Families and took lead responsibility for family policy from a variety of other government departments, including the Home Office and the DCA. She has responsibility for children and family policy including: children's social services; child protection; children in care; the Family Policy Unit (previously at the Home Office); family and parenting law; parental responsibility and the role of parents in supporting schools and family learning and extended schools. The DCA retained responsibility for areas such as divorce, since this falls primarily under the remit of the Court Service, and for the Legal Services Commission and the Community Legal Service. The Family Law and Mediation team at the LSC became part of a new Children and Family Services division. This division provides a central focus for all matters relating to children and families within the LSC. It reports to a programme board, made up of LSC, DCA and DfES representatives and the brief is to represent and take forward all matters pertaining to children, young people and their families. The intention is to allow unity of policies and ideas, eliminate duplication, and ensure harmonised communication. FAINs (see below) and mediation sit under the Children and Family Services umbrella and Angela Lake-Carroll, a mediator and mediation administrator of many years' standing is Head of the Division.

The Government agenda was to:

—   place children first;
—   protect children from harm;
—   ensure value for money via co-ordination of effort and services;
—   have equal access to services, advice and support;
—   reform the family justice system.

A DCA Family Insight Group had been working on reform of the family justice system with the aim of:

—   making the needs of children paramount;
—   improving education, information and advice easily available before, during, and after, relationship breakdown;
—   increasing the supply of mediation and support services to meet future demand;
—   having court resolution only when safety is an issue;
—   diverting divorce and financial disputes out of court to ADR;
—   encouraging court dispute resolution processes to be non-adversarial;
—   increasing supervised contact places;
—   successfully implementing court orders and enforcement.

A draft DCA manifesto specified:

—   working with the LSC to improve information advice and support made available by legal and other advisers to families in times of change;
—   working with the LSC to ensure that funding arrangements are built around customers' needs;
—   working with the legal profession, the judiciary, CAFCASS and consumers to provide opportunities for early and proportionate resolution of family disputes without recourse to the courts.

The LSC was:

—   working with the DCA Family Insight Group to help reduce the proportion of disputes which are resolved by resort to the courts (PSA target 3);
—   working within budget and ensuring that it secures value for money in its contracting arrangements (SR2004);
—   expanding FAINs to ensure that people have access to the appropriate services.

Lord Filkin, a Parliamentary Secretary in the DCA in his speech to the Solicitors Family Law Association (SFLA) annual conference in March 2004 described further the substantial amount of work with stakeholder groups, focus groups and the judiciary to assist the Government to think through what was needed to make the family justice system work better. He said it was a root and branch policy review and that the green paper would analyse the problems and give thoughts on improving the process. It would set out the 'direction of travel' for addressing those problems, even if the money was not available. The DCA would be in 'listening mode' to hear people's views.

As for the court system, the question for Government was what outcomes should the courts be delivering for the public and what sort of access to justice did it need to deliver, including the benefits of co-location of the county courts and family proceedings courts. There had been a reduction in the workload of the county courts – the number of Children Act applications fell from 17,000 in 1999 to 11,000 in 2003. One answer was to get the family proceedings courts working at their best capacity. But it was not simply a question about the court system and how it was structured but whether there should be better information for the public to deal with their own problems. Lord Filkin said there was an obvious benefit in being able to direct people more appropriately to ADR mechanisms.

So, the opportunity has arisen once again for the family mediation movement to come into its own, especially to make its own contribution to the plan rather than just be part of someone else's. The same opportunity arose during the lead up to the intended implementation of the Family Law Act 1996. At that time the family mediation movement was still obsessed with its own territoriality and allowed other interested forces to take the initiative and undermine the Act.

Back to the future

Gwynn Davis believes researchers are borderline psychopaths.[1] It is fitting that they should inform the politicians, who come from the same genetic pool. What were some of the research papers and events which engendered the thinking which led to the strategy and will inform the final conclusions and actions of the Government – apart from the obvious and overriding desire to save money? Will family mediation benefit from this wholesale Government re-think? First of all, will it benefit from the current malaise seriously affecting publicly funded lawyers?

At the beginning of 2004 the LSC faced heavy criticism about 'advice deserts' especially in February when, shortly after the Citizens Advice Bureaux produced a damning report, the *Law Society Gazette* published its third annual legal aid survey, which showed that 74 per cent of practitioners were ready to drop or cut back on the amount of legal aid work undertaken. More than nine out of 10 of the almost 300 firms that responded were dissatisfied with the system, and a similar number said they were more pessimistic than the previous year. Three-quarters of firms turned clients away in 2003 including a solicitor in Hampshire who was 'sending family cases to as far as 50 miles away'. There was pressure from the private side in many firms to drop legal aid, as it was seen as more trouble than it

---

[1] See Chapter 6, at p 59.

was worth. Family law emerged as one of the biggest problem areas; it was the most prevalent contract area for respondents to the survey (73 per cent had a family contract), and was also one of the areas most likely to operate alongside a large volume of privately funded work. In the year 2000 the LSC gave 4,286 family law contracts; this fell 16 per cent to 3,595 by 2003 although the number of matter starts in that period rose to 339,757. One family law solicitor with 17 years' experience wrote on his survey:

> 'I myself am no longer interested in doing legal aid work as there are no rewards for it, little monetary or [other] acknowledgement of the hard work and difficult circumstances to work in.'

The House of Commons' Constitutional Affairs Select Committee heard evidence on 'Civil Legal Aid: adequacy of provision' in April 2004.

The Legal Services Research Centre (LSRC), the independent research arm of the LSC, published, in February 2004, *Causes of Action: Civil Law and Social Justice* (TSO, 2004). For the research, 5,611 adults from a random 3,348 households in England and Wales were surveyed. The study revealed that, over a 3½-year period, more than one in three adults experienced a civil law problem; one in five took no action to solve their problem; and around 1 million problems go unsolved each year because people do not understand their basic rights or know how to seek help. The 18 problem categories included divorce, relationship breakdown, domestic violence, children, mental health, welfare benefits and money/debt. The research advocated a more joined-up and targeted government approach to civil law problems. The LSRC was also nearing the completion of Phase 2 of a 'Family Case Profiling Study'. The first study was completed in 1998. Phase 2 will establish whether the issue, parties and cost profiles of legally aided private family cases have changed since the original study was concluded. To this end, the project addressed the following questions:

- How are private family legally aided cases dealt with by solicitors?
- What are the cost, duration and end points of cases?
- What are the main cost drivers?
- What is the profile of the parties involved?
- To what extent has the behaviour of solicitors changed in relation to family law cases over the past 5 years?
- Has contracting private family work had an effect on solicitors' behaviour?
- What impact has the introduction of family mediation had on private family work?

The project was due to report in 2004.

The flowers destined to bloom in this desert are the LSC's Family Advice and Information Networks (FAINs). These have been piloted since 2002 and were designed to build on existing best practice in family law and existing support services in order to enable people to access a range of services through a single point of reference – initially, family lawyers. What might the FAINs services look like in the future? A clue came from Professor Janet Walker, research co-ordinator of the FAINs evaluation team who wrote in the June 2004 issue of *Family Law*:

'The researchers are aware that FAINs is developing against a background of increasing concern about legal aid rates (see research by Gwynn Davis, Steven Finch and Lee Barnham published at [2003] Fam Law 240 and 327). It seems clear that experienced family solicitors are withdrawing from legal aid work and re-allocating it to legal executives and more junior colleagues because the remuneration is seen as inadequate. In this respect, it seems essential that whole firms can be described as FAINs suppliers rather than restricting the label to a few more experienced practitioners. … It seems to us that if FAINs is looking to change legal practice, then it is more likely to succeed if whole family law departments in firms embrace the Commission's vision of holistic practice, and whole communities of divorce professionals examine new ways of working collaboratively.

The final report of the first Legal Services Research Centre's survey of justiciable problems (Pascoe Pleasance et al, 2004) refers to the 'advice maze' and an 'information black hole'. Many survey respondents did not know how to get the help they needed and few solicitors appeared to refer clients on. The researchers concluded that justiciable problems should be dealt with in the context of their causes and consequences and argue for greater coordination of advice and legal services and a more holistic approach to civil justice. Their study demonstrated that early and effective referral to the most appropriate agencies is an important component of an integrated approach. In the field of family law, FAINs would appear to offer an important opportunity to develop the kind of integrated approach which the LSRC study recommends.

Over the coming year, the research team will be monitoring the ongoing development of FAINs and the extent to which family law practice can embrace the Commission's holistic vision for supplying information and advice to publicly-funded clients.'[1]

The holistic approach was further promoted in the Government's response to *Making Contact Work* published in March 2004 which stated that the DCA was working with the LSC to ensure that the basis of legal aid funding responded to parents' needs for an expert early diagnosis of the key issues, for support in helping them to work things out themselves if possible or support for mediation if they needed that assistance. In April 2004 a DCA report *The Independent Review of the Community Legal Service* (Matrix) specifically recommended, with reference to changing the nature of LSC contracts with local providers, that the LSC pilot the commissioning of consortia of local providers to provide a 'one stop shop' for the provision of all early prevention, advice and publicly funded legal provision. In the same month the DCA report *Picking up the Pieces* (see below) mentioned a salaried scheme for publicly funded family lawyers based on a model from Alberta, Canada (where the number of lawyers prepared to take on publicly funded family work had also dropped). The Family Law Office (FLO) in Alberta provides a team approach to client services offering social as well as legal advice, emphasising alternative dispute resolution and mediation where possible. The 29 FLO lawyers work in small teams along with three family resource facilitators – two social workers and one psychologist – who work with the client and lawyer on

---

[1]   *FAINs – a New Approach for Family Lawyers?* [2004] Fam Law 436.

ancillary concerns such as financial assistance, shelter and housing, counselling, parenting and life skills. A database tracks clients as they are referred to other services and the lawyer case-manages the whole process. The LSC is already piloting a Public Defender Service which employs advocates who work only on publicly funded criminal defence cases.

Although mediation is clearly seen as one of the essential services for referral, will lawyers – or rather solicitors' practices – continue to be the gateway? Apparently not, as FAINs mediation gateways were expected to be operating from June 2004. Mediation services with LSC contracts had been invited to put forward ideas for becoming a FAINs access point. The FAINs model for mediators would not be the same as that which applied to FAINs solicitors As for the private family mediators, the FAINs culture will no doubt spread into that sector, assisted by whatever the DCA green paper revealed. Already non-FAINs solicitors are using the FAINs literature in their practices.

In *Picking up the Pieces: marriage and divorce two years after information provision* researchers at the Newcastle Centre for Family Studies followed up over a 30-month period participators in the pilot information meetings which took place from 1997–1999. The findings no doubt contributed to the development of DCA policy on providing information to divorcing couples and to the ongoing development of the FAINs. The study assessed what use people had made of the information they received, the decisions they had taken and the longer-term outcomes. At the time of its publication, Lord Filkin stated that the research addressed a number of key themes that bore on the initiatives the Government were taking forward in support of the principles underlying the Family Law Act 1996: saving marriages, promoting conciliatory divorce and encouraging positive relationships between children and separated parents. The holistic approach was once more stressed in that report:

> 'However well-intentioned people are as regards managing the process of separation and divorce in as amicable a way as possible, the research shows that it is rare for the transition from marriage to divorce to be without conflict at some time or other. Few people in the study chose to use mediation as a way of resolving disputes, however, and those who did were often critical about the service they received. There were criticisms, too, of the way some solicitors dealt with matters. The findings suggest that more attention needs to be given to the processes people go through and to finding ways of ameliorating the emotional distress they experience. An excessive focus on outcomes does little to help people achieve a more conciliatory divorce and work together to develop better relationships in the future. The follow-up study confirms the value of providing comprehensive information for couples facing difficulties in their relationship, of ensuring that divorce professionals such as counsellors, mediators and lawyers are able to offer appropriate support and advice, and of focusing on helping parents to develop and maintain loving and responsible relationships.'

Before mediators get too smug about the solicitors, the research also stated that 'satisfaction with solicitors was higher than satisfaction with mediators, but not as high as satisfaction with counsellors'. Only 10 per cent of survey respondents had attended mediation. Fourteen per cent of mediation users, most of whom had been referred by a solicitor, seemed unclear about why they were going to mediation at all. Sixty-two per cent left mediation with unresolved issues and 25 per cent resolved all the issues they had raised in the mediation process.

Perhaps the only consolation is that from 1997–1999 when the information meetings were being piloted, and when Gwynn Davis was conducting his research into mediation for the LSC, mediators were not quite up to speed on financial mediation or getting agreements. Hopefully, having had more practice over the last 5 years, we are doing better now in terms of outcomes. The Government Response to *Making Contact Work*, published in 2004 stated, more encouragingly, that the number of publicly funded mediations supported by the LSC had increased from 400 in 1997/98 to over 12,000 in 2001/2. Just over half of the mediations commenced in 2001/2 involved dealing with both financial issues and disputes about children. Approximately 60 per cent of mediations undertaken resulted in full agreement on the issues in dispute.

Other studies have suggested that divorcing couples do not often consult a solicitor early in the separation process, and that cohabiting couples are less likely to consult one at all.[1] In the September 2004 issue of *Family Law* Moorhead, Douglas, Sefton and Doughty, reporting on research from Cardiff Law School, state that lone parents wrestle with advice mazes and advice deserts. Many struggle to know where to go for advice, and find it difficult to find someone able to see them face to face or talk to them on the telephone:

> 'The study has highlighted some fundamental issues facing family policy makers. First, regardless of family form, all families face problems and may need help when relationships break down. But it is clear that family form partly determines the extent to which advice is sought and the avenues of help which are followed – those who have been married are, for example, more likely to seek help from solicitors than those who have not. With marriage in decline and ever increasing numbers of cohabiting and never-together parents, it is becoming inappropriate, unfair and inefficient to focus advice and support so dominantly on lawyers and a legal system which many of those facing the greatest challenges will never think to access. There are therefore question marks over whether solicitors should have the pivotal role in acting as the initial referral points for FAINs. It is heartening, then, to know that the LSC have begun to realise this in their analysis of how FAINs should be developed in the future, with mediators and others being brought in as initial contact points.'[2]

The Funding Code

Family mediation relies heavily on the LSC, and not only in the 'not-for-profit' sector. Annual mediation starts under the LSC Family Mediation Contracts, taken from the LSC annual report 2002/2003 were:

2000/2001	9,309
2001/2002	12,235
2002/2003	13,841
2003/2004 (estimate)	14,561

---

[1] A Perry et al, *How Parents Cope Financially on Divorce* (Joseph Rowntree Foundation, 2000); S Arthur, *Setting Up* (NCSR, 2000); A Moorman, *Understanding Parents' Needs* (NFPI, 2001).

[2] 'The Advice Needs of Lone Parents' [2004] Fam Law [September issue].

There were, within the publicly funded sector, about 72,000 certificates issued in 2002/3 to cases which might otherwise have been susceptible to mediation and there were 21,141 publicly funded mediation clients. We need the LSC but do they need us? Giving evidence to Parliament's Constitutional Affairs Committee in September 2003, Clare Dodgson, the LSC chief executive said:

> 'I think we have got some very real questions to ask ourselves and answer about mediation. Certainly I have been talking to a lot of groups that are not just the Law Society or the Legal Aid Practitioners' Group – as have many of my colleagues including my chairman – to say what is the role of mediation, what is the role of the not-for-profit sector, what is the role for organisations like the Citizens' Advice Bureau? How do we work with other government agencies? There is a real role for us to start working with other government departments and other agencies because many of the clients are the same people. They are people who are vulnerable, disadvantaged, very often their lifestyles are chaotic, and if we can start with the individuals, their families and their communities and then build our services around them – I use the term 'wrap the service around the individual' rather than 'salami slice' the person into the services – then I genuinely believe we have got a job to be done.'

Philip Ely, the LSC chairman, and former President of the Law Society, added:

> 'On the question of mediation, I think one has to say that has been a long haul. I happened to notice that your last witness was Lord Mackay, the former Lord Chancellor, and I recall that a decade ago when he was Lord Chancellor he was particularly anxious to drive forward mediation in family work. I think enormous progress has been made, and it is easy to say that I think the understanding of the role of mediation is coming up the agenda, but it is a long time. Our own pilots in relation to family, the FAINs pilot and the FAINs work, has taken time. Again, I am sorry to be negative, but I do not think one can do it for less, I think one has to develop and evolve it in that way and it is in with a chance.'

Are s 29 referrals (as now implemented via s 11 of the Funding Code together with the Funding Code Procedures and Guidance) under threat? Whilst David Emmerson, then Chair of the Legal Aid Practitioners Group, in 'The Future for Family Legal Aid' [2003] Fam Law 765 understandably looked for cuts in the family legal aid budget that would not directly affect lawyers, family mediators do not want to see compulsory referrals under the Funding Code scrapped. Some services have consistently 'converted' just under 50 per cent of all referrals into mediation in the last 5 years. The compulsory s 29 referral is the mechanism that has substantially raised awareness of mediation and is mainly responsible for the growth of family mediation work. (How s 29 sits alongside FAINs is an interesting question, especially as in the pilot areas s 29 was suspended.)

Robin ap Cynan, Chairman of the Law Society's Family Mediation Panel, has summarised improvements to s 29 whereby it could become more of a joint convening meeting than a solo information-giving and legal-aid-gateway meeting. He has suggested that modification was required to the existing Funding Code referral mechanism to require legally aided respondents to court proceedings to attend a mediation assessment meeting before the proceedings could continue and possibly jointly with the applicant. Proper information could be given and received and proper consideration given as to what dispute resolution mechanism might be jointly selected. A similar mechanism might also assist in the diversion of privately funded disputants away from the courts. In addition:

(i)   Section 29 might be biting at the wrong time; a better time to require proper consideration of mediation might be either immediately before or immediately after the issue of proceedings (ie children or ancillary relief proceedings, not the divorce itself), at the same time as the obligation arose upon the respondent to engage with the proceedings.

(ii)   That would be especially helpful given that there was no existing mechanism to compel the respondent to proceedings to come to the second half of a s 29 meeting. Such a requirement could usefully be introduced, particularly if the biting point of a s 29 referral were shifted to a more appropriate time adjacent to the issue of proceedings.

(iii)   There should be mechanisms for applying a s 29 style referral mechanism on other occasions in addition to the start.

(iv)   There should be a clear protocol for judicial referral to a convening or s 29 style mediation assessment meeting.

Contracting with family mediation suppliers

The family mediation pilot started in May 1997 and standard contracts with the 'for-profit' suppliers came into force in December 2002. Until October 2004 'not-for-profit' providers had individual pilot contracts but the LSC wanted to introduce standard contracts which would cover payment, standard terms and conditions and reporting work. The objectives of the new payment model are:

–   to provide incentives for services to increase their volumes of work;
–   to ensure that services have a predictable income stream to assist them with future planning;
–   to link payments to volumes of work undertaken;
–   to ensure that there is a balance between maintaining access to services and having more cost effective and efficient services;
–   to have one standard contract within 3 years – the transitional model.

The contracts will therefore eventually be the same as the 'for-profit' providers'. The LSC had already stressed the importance of the voluntary and community sector taking a strategic and holistic view of funding, whether seeking to increase capacity or to maintain current service levels. It had even put together an overview of the main funding sources, together with details of websites to take managers through the funding maze. How 'not-for-profit' services meet these challenges remains to be seen.

Alternatives to public funding

Eligibility for legal aid is bound to get more restricted, if not for children issues then definitely for ancillary relief. (That said, would so many intractable contact cases end up before the courts if one side were not publicly funded?) The fact that wives in moderately wealthy marriages can be legally aided seems peculiar to some. The whole issue of ancillary relief was at the time of writing under the scrutiny of the President's Ancillary Relief Action Group which would be recommending rule changes to the DCA. With regard to costs it is possible that the reasonable costs of each party will be treated as part of that party's liabilities or reasonable needs. This could mean that, as standard practice, the payment of both parties' costs would be a first claim on the matrimonial assets before division.

Maybe the LSC will adopt a student loans type scheme or follow the example of the public defender service pilots. Another scheme was highlighted in Freedman and Russell, 'The Search for a Solution to Divorce Funding'.[1] A 'divorce loan' is offered by Alternative Matrimonial and Litigation Funding Ideas (Amalfi), created in conjunction with private bank Leopold Joseph & Sons. The scheme works like an overdraft: no funds are paid until the divorce case is settled and the loan incurs interest at 7 per cent above base rate, currently 10.5 per cent. Either spouse can take out a loan of up to £50,000, in stages, using the money to pay legal bills as and when they arise, rather than borrowing the whole sum at once. Interest is only paid on what has been borrowed so far. Clients have up to 2 years before repaying – at least until the family home is sold or the assets have been divided. There are no redemption penalties if the debt is cleared sooner rather than later.

Judicial mediation management

The present family justice regime does little to divert privately funded family disputants away from the courts. Hopefully, the DCA green paper will have addressed this deficiency. It is impossible to make any sort of accurate estimate of the number of current privately funded mediations but probably rather less than one in 20, or less than 5 per cent of privately funded work, is resolved via mediation, and possibly fewer than 2 per cent is mediated. What is required is a mechanism within the family field similar to that within the Civil Procedure Rules requiring a consideration of ADR and/or family mediation. For a start, diversionary tactics implemented and controlled by members of the family judiciary could be put into place analogous to the civil mediation projects at Exeter County Court and elsewhere in Devon. As Emma Harte, Chair of the SFLA Mediation Committee and Helen Howard, an SFLA mediation trainer, wrote in the June 2004 issue of *Family Law*:

> 'The commercial litigation field has witnessed a revolution in recent years. No longer can a commercial litigant dismiss mediation – it is financial suicide casually to reject an offer to mediate without reason. Costs penalties arising out of a refusal or failure to attempt mediation have concentrated commercial lawyers' minds on mediation referrals and created an explosion in cases for commercial mediators. Why are there not similar sanctions as far as family law is concerned, perhaps combined with incentives to consider mediation as a first, rather than last, resort?
>
> ... The time may have come to abandon the dearly held principle of voluntary mediation ...'

---

[1]   [2003] Fam Law 769.

Professor Hazel Genn, in *Court-Based Initiatives for Non-Family Civil Disputes: The Commercial Court and the Court of Appeal*,[1] noted that the success rate of court-ordered ancillary dispute resolution (ADR) over the review period settled at around 50 per cent, but even where ADR was unsuccessful, the great majority of cases subsequently settled with only a tiny minority of cases proceeding to trial. *CEDR Solve* reported in 2004 that the Commercial Court of Appeal mediation scheme has been doing even better, with a settlement rate of about 77 per cent. Court-directed mediation can, and does, work. Moreover it provides an important positive message that the courts expect parties to behave responsibly and settle wherever possible.

Could the judiciary be more proactive in encouraging parents to resolve problems through mediation backed up by costs penalties commercial style if an offer to mediate is unreasonably refused? Anecdotally (there appears to be no case-law on the point), the provisions of the Family Law Protocol about promoting mediation have not been given teeth via costs orders against solicitors who refuse, without even giving reasons, to refer to mediation. The ancillary relief rules, as defined by the Family Proceedings Rules 1991[2] amended by the Family Proceedings Rules 1991,[3] set out a procedural code "with the overriding objective of enabling the court to deal with cases justly". Rule 2.51B provides for the court to further the overriding objective by actively managing cases including "encouraging the parties to settle their disputes through mediation where appropriate". Rule 2.61D, relating to the first appointment, provides for the court to, among other options, direct 'that the case be adjourned for out-of-court mediation or private negotiation' where a referral to a financial dispute resolution appointment is not appropriate. The latent powers appear to have been little used thus far.[4]

The judiciary could already do more. I have sat all day in the mediators' room at Slough County Court waiting for lawyers or the district judge to send me Children Act 1989 clients. Another day I have seen three couples in a morning. It all depended on the judge's attitude to mediation on the day. To overcome this lottery a protocol supported by a Practice Direction requiring a mediation referral before matters can proceed could be made applicable to all levels of family courts. We only have to look to ss 13 and 14 of the Family Law Act 1996 (not yet repealed) for a precedent:

13.—(1) After the court has received a statement, it may give a direction requiring each party to attend a meeting arranged in accordance with the direction for the purpose –
(a) of enabling an explanation to be given of the facilities available to the parties for mediation in relation to disputes between them; and
(b) of providing an opportunity for each party to agree to take advantage of those facilities.

(2) A direction may be given at any time, including in the course of proceedings connected with the breakdown of the marriage (as to which see section 25).

---

[1] LCD Research Series 2002.
[2] SI 1991/1247.
[3] SI 1999/3491.
[4] 'Encouraging Positive Parental Relationships: Time for Carrots and Sticks?' [2004] Fam Law 455.

(3)   A direction may be given on the application of either of the parties or on the initiative of the court.

(4)   The parties are to be required to attend the same meeting unless –
         (a) one of them asks, or both of them ask, for separate meetings; or
         (b) the court considers separate meetings to be more appropriate.

(5)   A direction shall –
         (a) specify a person chosen by the court (with that person's agreement) to arrange and conduct the meeting or meetings; and
         (b) require such person as may be specified in the direction to produce to the court, at such time as the court may direct, a report stating –
             (i)   whether the parties have complied with the direction; and
             (ii)   if they have, whether they have agreed to take part in any mediation.

14.—(1) The court's power to adjourn any proceedings connected with the breakdown of a marriage includes power to adjourn –
         (a) for the purpose of allowing the parties to comply with a direction under section 13; or
         (b) for the purpose of enabling disputes to be resolved amicably.

(2)   In determining whether to adjourn for either purpose, the court shall have regard in particular to the need to protect the interests of any child of the family.

(3)   If the court adjourns any proceedings connected with the breakdown of a marriage for either purpose, the period of the adjournment must not exceed the maximum period prescribed by rules of court.

(4)   Unless the only purpose of the adjournment is to allow the parties to comply with a direction under section 13, the court shall order one or both of them to produce to the court a report as to –
         (a)   whether they have taken part in mediation during the adjournment;
         (b)   whether, as a result, any agreement has been reached between them;
         (c)   the extent to which any dispute between them has been resolved as a result of any such agreement;
         (d)   the need for further mediation
         (e)   how likely it is that further mediation will be successful.'

Some courts do have a referral system and coherent approach – as Roger Bird has demonstrated in Bristol (see p 54), likewise in Exeter and the Principal Registry. There are similar initiatives in all levels of courts, including the Court of Appeal where, thanks to the continuing support of Lord Justice Thorpe, it has been agreed that a family mediation referral scheme will be administered by the UK College of Family Mediators so that all Court of Appeal family work can in the first instance be directed to the mediation process if suitable. It is hoped to extend the scheme to the Family Division. It is also what many judges want. For example, when in April 2004 an exasperated Mr Justice Munby gave the media his judgment in

Re D (Intractable Contact Dispute: Publicity),[1] he said that the two great vices of the present system for deciding contact and residence were:

- that the system was, for all practical purposes, still almost exclusively court based; and
- that the court's procedures were not working, and not working as speedily and efficiently, as they could be and therefore as they should be.

He made several suggestions as to what should be done as a matter of urgency, focusing on what the judges could do themselves without either legislation or additional funding: 'What is needed – all that is needed – is a protocol supported by a President's Practice Direction'. He said that delay was the scourge of the family justice system. The *Protocol for Judicial Case Management in Public Law Children Cases* had addressed the problems in relation to public law cases in its intent to reduce delay by judicial continuity and case management: 'I see no reason why comparable principles should not be applied in relation to all but the simplest or most straightforward private law cases'. What was needed was a consistent judicial approach in relation to:

- separate representation of the children;
- independent social workers who could remain with children long enough to form a long-term relationship;
- experts and other outside agencies who could help facilitate contact rather than writing reports;
- allegations of misconduct which should be speedily investigated and resolved, not left to fester unresolved as a continuing source of friction and dispute;
- a clear and hard-headed approach to the timetable.

He added

> 'Some will be disappointed – and I can understand why – that the Government's very recently announced [family resolutions project] pilot-scheme proposals only encourage the use of mediation and do not make it mandatory. The sooner we can get to a situation where as many contact disputes as possible are removed from the courtroom setting the better.'

In May 2004 Mrs Justice Bracewell reinforced the judiciary's attitude in *V v V*[2] where the court found that the mother had consistently undermined and thwarted the father's contact with the children, making serious unsubstantiated allegations against him and his family in order to frustrate contact, subjecting the children to emotional abuse in the process. She noted that, although the current difficulties with intractable contact disputes could be remedied in part by procedural improvements in the court process such as judicial continuity, case management, timetabling and pro-active orders, with early effective intervention by officers of CAFCASS, there was also a need for legislation giving the judiciary powers to

---

[1]   [2004] 1 FLR 1226.
[2]   [2004] 2 FLR 851.

enforce orders for contact, by enabling judges and magistrates to refer parties to mediation or to a psychiatrist at any stage.

By October 2004 the DCA green paper should have made proposals in this area, the Unified Courts Administration will be starting to integrate the family courts and the Family Justice Council will have begun to introduce a new era of inter-disciplinarity.

CAFCASS

A major player in the future of family mediation will be the Children and Family Court Advisory and Support Service (CAFCASS) which has had its downs and downs but which, with a new Chair and a new Board appointed in April 2004, can now aspire to be part of the solution, rather than the problem. The current strategy 'includes close partnership with others within the family justice system to meet the needs of the children and families who pass through it and to meet the requirements of the European Convention on Human Rights. We wish to create a learning organisation with a confident, valued workforce; to see CAFCASS contributing to the wider children agenda; growing into a role in which it provides a range of support to children and families as well as reports to courts. There are exciting challenges ahead of us, not least in private law where we are looking forward to consulting on the contact guidelines and to playing our part in the Family Resolutions Pilot.[1]

Will CAFCASS work in conjunction with the out-of-court services or will it concentrate on in-court schemes manned by its own staff? Before the white knight of public funding rode over the mediation horizon in 1996, a significant portion of financial support came to 'not-for-profit' services from local court welfare offices. In 2001, 22 per cent of CAFCASS partnerships were with mediation services and they received 61 per cent of the partnership budget. Some 'not-for-profit' mediators provided, and still do, efficient in-court services. Will CAFCASS continue to farm out mediation work or will CAFCASS officer in-court mediation be a more effective – and cheaper – alternative?

In March 2004 the Government published its response to the Lord Chancellor's Advisory Board on Family Law report, *Making Contact Work*[2] concerning contact between parents and children following divorce or separation. The response stated that CAFCASS had done a significant amount of dispute resolution work with parents at directions appointments in private law, making 42,000 interventions in the year to March 2003. Insufficient research was available on outcomes but small studies had shown (eg Mantle, 'A Consumer Survey of Agreements Reached in County Court Dispute Resolution (Mediation, 2002) that agreement rates could compare favourably with out-of-court mediation. In *Seeking Agreement* published in December 2003 the Magistrates' Courts Services Inspectorate (MCSI) reported on the operation of schemes involving CAFCASS at an early stage of private law proceedings and recommended further research.

---

[1]   Baroness Pitkeathley, Chair of CAFCASS [2004] Fam Law 475.
[2]   DCA, 2003.

In *Making Contact Work* the Government announced a 'Family Resolution Pilot'. Based in London, Brighton and the North East the aim was to divert families from court to mediation. Parents would not be compelled to take part in the pilot but judges could question why they had not taken the opportunity. The pilot was to be jointly run by the DCA and the DfES. The response clearly stated that CAFCASS and DfES would be looking to see if there was scope for extending the availability of such work, with the assistance of the MCSI, national bodies and the voluntary sector. The pilot proposed that both parents attended one-to-one sessions to agree a parenting plan, which, if necessary, could be ratified by the judge. Instead of waiting 10–16 weeks for the first hearing, parents would be able to meet a family mediator to discuss contact within 2 weeks. A similar scheme has been operating in parts of the USA .where parents have been successfully involved in participating in the resolution of contract disputes outside the courts, but as *Making Contact Work* points out, 'This may well be a reflection not only of the regard with which US citizens regard their legal system, but also with the fact that they are obliged to fund their own legal expenses'. The pilot takes as its starting point work carried out by an ad hoc group of judges, legal professionals and other interested parties in the UK to test alternative means of resolving contact disputes informed by the USA experience, including:

–   diversion of parents to the scheme on a voluntary basis at the court application stage, providing information about the pilot and an immediate referral;
–   screening for domestic violence/abuse at the initial stage, with judicial consideration and risk assessment taking place as relevant;
–   parental attendance at information and support sessions focusing on co-parenting and the child's needs; and
–   family resolution sessions which aim to help the parents produce an agreed timetabled plan which sets out how they will co-operate about the future parenting of their children.

The pilots are to run for one year.

Regulation

Family mediators are, in effect, regulated by the UK College of Family Mediators, the Law Society and in their publicly funded activities by the LSC. Regulation is well documented elsewhere in this book (see Thelma Fisher at Chapter 7). The Government is apparently content to leave regulation to market forces and the only likely change will affect lawyer-mediators in the shape of the Clementi Report. Sir David Clementi was appointed by the Secretary of State for Constitutional Affairs in 2003 to review how lawyers and other providers of legal advice are regulated. His consultation paper published in March 2004 suggested either a Legal Services Authority, replacing all regulatory functions of the professional bodies, taking over training and setting professional standards as well as handling complaints and discipline: alternatively a Legal Services Board acting as a super-regulator or umbrella body that would delegate regulatory functions to the Law Society and Bar Council. The consultation period ended in June 2004 and Clementi's recommendations are due to be published at the end of 2004.

The contribution, both past and continuing, of the Law Society to the growth of family mediation should not be underestimated. The aims and objectives of the Family Advice and Information Service (FAINs) are clearly consistent with the thinking encompassed in the Law Society's Family Law Protocol. Indeed, it could be argued that the FAINs offer a national endorsement of that Protocol, providing a timely vehicle by which it could be fully operationalised. About 40 lawyer-mediators have set up successful mediation-only practices and a further 100–200 work part time. The Law Society's Family Mediation Panel was officially launched in February 2004 and defines a rigorous path for training and accreditation. The SFLA mediation committee is one of the most active promoters of family mediation in the UK. Both have had influential input into the Government thinking outlined above. To divide family mediators into lawyers and non-lawyers is, in itself, a retrograde trap into which I have just fallen. Both have learnt – and continue to learn – from each other and clients would be often hard pressed to tell the difference, apart from looking round their offices.

The downside is the waste of lawyer-mediator talent because of lack of referrals. Roughly 200–400 mediators average only 6 cases per year and 500–800 have been trained but do not practice. Some will have not been assessed as competent either by the LSC/UK College competence assessment procedure nor can they demonstrate their competence by reference to membership of the Law Society Family Mediation Panel. Solicitor family mediation capacity will continue to contract unless the amount of publicly and privately funded family mediation suddenly increases.

This investment in time and training fees might be saved by collaborative law which is an ADR model from the USA and Canada. It depends on lawyers assisting the search for fair, interest-based solutions and gives clients access to legal advice throughout the process. It generally involves negotiations advancing in four-way meetings at which clients, assisted by the lawyers, who are committed to a transparent search for fair solutions, identify problems, identify possible solutions and reality-test them. Collaborative law may include referral to, for example, an external mediator, counsellor, child specialist or financial adviser to assist with the process. It seems to provide that combination of legal advice and mediation which can frustrate many clients in mediation who cannot, understandably, understand why they keep being sent off to lawyers in between sessions, paying over again for a similar (to them) service. Collaborative family practice might fit well with a FAINs approach since it encourages solicitors to adopt an enhanced role with their clients, orchestrating processes that can be tailored to particular situations and concerns.

Europe

The progress of family mediation in the USA, Australia and New Zealand has been well documented. What is the attitude to mediation in the EU? The greatest triumph for the UK was the Council of Europe's 1998 conference devoted to family mediation when the UK College was able to demonstrate the UK as being a leader in the field. The Lord Chancellor, Lord Irvine, gave the closing address and was well briefed on the UK's achievements. Eight months later he dropped the 1996 Act. Greater commitment has been shown in other areas, for example:

–   In 2002 Reunite launched a mediation pilot scheme for child abduction, limited initially to England, Ireland and France. Mediation takes place during the course of a court-endorsed adjournment of the proceedings over a maximum of 5 days.
–   The new European Commission Brussels II regulation on parental responsibility, which will come into force in March 2005, establishes a system of central authorities across the EC which must co-operate in specific cases to assist holders of parental responsibility and facilitate their agreement through mediation or other means.
–   In May 2004 the DCA published a consultation paper seeking views on whether the UK should sign and ratify the Council of Europe Convention on Contact Concerning Children. The Convention requires States to encourage parents and other persons having family ties with the child to comply with its principles in making agreements concerning contact.
–   The European Commission published a green paper on ADR in 2002 as a response to Member States' governments who produced legislation encouraging ADR. It highlights in particular ADR as a means of improving access to justice.
–   A Netherlands Government research project has provided mediation training to 500 judges and offered mediation in slightly different formats in five courts. Judges, court staff, users of the scheme and their legal advisers were interviewed over a period of 3 years, and the results were evaluated. The findings are that:
    –   61 per cent of those undertaking mediation reached an agreement;
    –   most parties were satisfied with mediation, even if no agreement was reached;
    –   parties liked mediation in cases where they wanted to:
        –   take responsibility for their own solutions;
        –   save costs;
        –   save time.

In Holland, all cases have a 'settlement conference' at some stage during the litigation process, and many of the cases referred to mediation during the project were referred after the settlement conference. As a result of the Netherlands pilot, an integrated system of litigation, arbitration and mediation will be rolled out across the country, with the aim of helping people choose the process that will be most appropriate to their case.

Any other business

There are many opportunities for family mediators to develop their skills. Some clients would prefer to present the memorandum of understanding directly to the court, especially if they do not have to pay a solicitor to draw up a consent order. As long as both parties agree to waive their privilege, why not? As the number of litigants in person increases, the judiciary might even welcome it. Many mediation services are delivering child counselling and pre-court assessments and others wish to develop contact centre provision. In another area the DfES consultation on special guardianship, to be introduced under the Adoption and Children Act 2002, specifies that local authorities will have to arrange for the provision of support services including mediation. In 'The Mediator as Midwife – a Marketing Opportunity',[1] Professor Chris Barton, Vice President of the Family Mediators Association, suggested that mediators became part of the pre-marriage/cohabitation process, helping the couple to draw up proposals 'to help prospective partners to improve prospects for their coupledom'. Family mediators are already moving into the housing and neighbourhood fields. It is of note that National Family Mediation has joined forces with Mediation UK. It is not easy, however, to find the time to break free from LSC restrictions and out-of-date codes of practice. Probably many family mediators are being inventive but wisely choose to keep it to themselves.

The mediators

It is, however, fruitless to hypothesise about the future of mediation and ignore the future of family mediators. What keeps us at work now and from where will new mediators be recruited? UK College membership has fallen from over 1,000 in 1999 to 700 in 2004. National Family Mediation has 542 mediators on its books and SFLA 250, which more or less adds up to the UK College figure. About 50 new mediators per year are currently assessed for competence by the UK College for LSC purposes.

There are still many mediators who have been practising for 10 years or more. They have lived through the highs of the advent of public funding and the prospect of the Family Law Act 1996 and the lows of tedious s 29 intakes and LSC bureaucracy. Not-for-profit mediators are lucky to earn more than £22 an hour and solicitor-mediators may not even get the work. Very few are earning a living from mediation. The only ones who are have devoted considerable time and energy in building up a private practice, are managers in the 'not-for-profit sector', or are supervisors/consultants who have succeeded in hoarding customers. All are reliant on public funding to a greater or lesser degree. The real winners are the trainers, but they have always done well.

The way ahead for mediators might lie within a general qualification for all mediators. The ADR Group already runs a conversion course and the UK College is exploring a possible 'equivalence' between qualifications in different mediation fields. A trained family mediator would be well advised as a career move to join other sectors which are better paid. A private family mediation service for which I worked briefly now takes on highly profitable work-place mediation with public companies and government departments.

But if this book has a use while delving into the past, it surely is to have learnt from history. The opportunity for unification of the profession of family mediation was there for the taking in the 2 years before the 1996 Act was shelved. Now is the time for all mediators to grab that opportunity again, before other forces and interests take the initiative and the ear of Government.

---

[1]   [2003] Fam Law 195.